WORDSEARCH
ENGLISH

WORDSEARCH
ENGLISH

The Fun Way to Learn the Language

SIRIUS

SIRIUS

This edition published in 2023 by Sirius Publishing, a division of
Arcturus Publishing Limited,
26/27 Bickels Yard, 151–153 Bermondsey Street,
London SE1 3HA

ISBN: 978-1-3988-2912-1
AD010957UK

Printed in China

Introduction

Hello and welcome to this book of more than 100 wonderful wordsearch puzzles, designed to be a fun way to help you learn the English language! Whether you are a complete novice wanting to learn a few words before a trip, a learner looking for a new way to expand your knowledge, or are just in need of a refresher in the language, you're sure to learn a lot as you enjoy solving the puzzles inside. You can also use them as a fun way to help your children to learn English!

While not a comprehensive guide to learning English, nor a replacement for a phrasebook or tuition, this book is intended to be an entertaining way to build your vocabulary and expand your knowledge of all things English. The wordsearches within contain English vocabulary and phrases on useful topics such as greetings, getting around, and shopping. Each word or phrase has space beneath it for you to write the translation in your own language, should you wish to, to help you remember what it means. If you want to translate a phrase rather than just the capitalized word, you may find it helpful to use a notepad as well as this book. Alongside the vocabulary-building puzzles are fun wordsearches filled with trivia from English-speaking countries, such as top tourist attractions, writers, and musicians.

Why learn English?

English is a global language, spoken by millions of people all over the world. It is the international language of science, academia, and business, and the most-used language online. Knowing at least a little English will increase your chance of being able to communicate with people wherever you are and will also allow you to enjoy the huge array of films, books, and music that are produced in English.

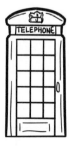

A few basic tips as you embark on your English adventure

English grammar is relatively simple. Unlike many other languages, it is mostly gender-neutral, with simple plurals and straightforward verb conjugations. However, the fact that English has its roots in many languages and has developed over centuries has led to it containing irregularities and quirks, and that's where practice with a book like this can help, with real-life examples of the language as you will use it.

The word order of a sentence is used to determine the relationship between the words in it. Every sentence must have a subject and a verb and in a simple sentence the subject comes first, followed by the verb and then sometimes an object (**The cat eats**, or **the cat eats the food**).

The subject and the verb must agree in number, and verbs change (are conjugated) depending on the subject (e.g., **I** *am* **happy**, **you** *are* **happy**, **they** *are* **happy**).

An adjective generally comes before the noun and doesn't change in English depending on what it is describing, unlike in many other languages.

The definite article is always **the** in English. The indefinite article is **a** before a consonant sound and **an** before a vowel sound.

The puzzles

To solve the puzzles, all you need to do is find the capitalized, italicized words within the grids. They can run in any direction, including diagonally. Now you are all set to start solving the puzzles and learning useful English words and phrases as you go. Have fun!

Note: some words differ between UK and US English, and where this is the case, this book shows both, for example **Films** (UK)/**movies** (US).

Essential Words and Phrases

```
F S R V G Y Y K F K N D W I A
V P L E H A R W N W I B Y R T
E G O O D N I G H T E M H N A
M M E D C G H O G E L Y O U R
A E O F Y O N N D N R P W J R
N O L L W R I I O U L E A T G
G S Z M A N R O N I F I R Z F
R I U G R R N O K E B R E T E
C C P O J R M E S S V R Y D E
H D M L E X C U S E M E O J M
L U G T E T H A N K Y O U O O
A Y F A E A J C E M I T L E C
T A D I N S S T E E M L N S L
E N G L I S H E B I E I E H E
R Z G O O D B Y E H F S I A W
```

HELLO.	See you *LATER.*	Can you *HELP* me?
GOODBYE.	You are *WELCOME.*	I would *LIKE* …
Have a *GOOD DAY.*	*EXCUSE ME.*	At what *TIME* is …?
Good *MORNING.*	*SORRY.*	*WHERE* can I …?
Good *AFTERNOON.*	If you *PLEASE.*	*HOW MUCH* is …?
Good *EVENING.*	*THANK YOU* very much.	Do you speak *ENGLISH*?
GOODNIGHT.	*HOW ARE YOU*?	My *NAME* is …
I am pleased to *MEET* you.	I'm *FINE*, thank you.	What is *YOUR* name?

Understanding

```
A V P A Y E B N E K R L V N A
K F E L O D O A A T N Z S I V
D V C V E L H E T L I K T A A
W O N K A A P M L Y N R E L I
B L U B D S S F M I R M W T L
E D O O D Y M E R F T R B D A
C U N R E N G L I S H T O I B
T O O S E L A E R G H G L S L
T B R L O P P T M A L B C E E
J O P O N G E I S E R N B M G
T N Z W Z N H A B R S F K H R
R D E L L A C D T I E U Z I B
S I K Y M F T Y E D V D C Y R
O O L R H C P S G E U S N X T
V R E T E R P R E T N I U U E
```

Do you speak *ENGLISH*?

....

Does anyone *SPEAK* English?

....

I *DO NOT* speak English.

....

I speak a *LITTLE* English.

....

I *NEED* an *INTERPRETER*.

....

EXCUSE ME.

....

What does … *MEAN*?

....

Do you *UNDERSTAND*?

....

How do you *PRONOUNCE* …?

....

How do you *WRITE* …?

....

Could you *REPEAT* that?

....

Could you *PLEASE* write that down?

....

Could you please speak more *SLOWLY*?

....

I do not *KNOW*.

....

SORRY.

....

What is that *CALLED*?

....

Can you tell me *ABOUT* …?

....

Is this *AVAILABLE* in English?

....

Numbers

```
D W H D I U W M B C N Z F A W
G N E T C S T S O O E K P A D
I I B A T T O F I R E E U D N
L T U O W G M L O I U T K G A
O L N T O F L I A R W E D C S
T E I H C I N D O E T U T V U
H B U R M G E E N R B Y M I O
G L I E S R R T V E P C K F H
I C H E D P Y D L E S I A I T
E O T N N W I V R E L F R V O
V W U H U E J V Y A V E O E Y
F H R G I N V J T H D L E U N
J C I X P R I E M L D S E A R
U I I J P M T N S A T E A W I
T S M N B N W Y E F I F T Y T
```

ZERO

....

ONE

....

TWO

....

THREE

....

FOUR

....

FIVE

....

SIX

....

SEVEN

....

EIGHT

....

NINE

....

TEN

....

ELEVEN

....

TWELVE

....

TWENTY

....

THIRTY

....

FORTY

....

FIFTY

....

HUNDRED

....

THOUSAND

....

MILLION

....

The Calendar

```
F J V Z Y D E C E M B E R C N
W T K L O M Y S A Y V R Y O Z
U E U F R A P R U M S O A C V
O J D M D R C T G O F E D T P
K Y K N I H G U U K J S S O N
B A O N E F K E S Y A R R B O
S M G L J S G S T A N E U E V
F U L Y R F D D K D U B H R E
E F M P A V U A T N A M T N M
B R U M R D R Y Y U R E Z O B
R I Y O E G R A T S Y T N F E
U D W D T R P U E P L P P U R
A A U O N R M L T Y F E B G J
R Y G H I N R B L A I S C Z M
Y Y P L W K M M F I S O J N Y
```

MONDAY	*FEBRUARY*	*OCTOBER*
TUESDAY	*MARCH*	*NOVEMBER*
WEDNESDAY	*APRIL*	*DECEMBER*
THURSDAY	*MAY*	*SPRING*
FRIDAY	*JUNE*	*SUMMER*
SATURDAY	*JULY*	*AUTUMN / fall*
SUNDAY	*AUGUST*	*WINTER*
JANUARY	*SEPTEMBER*	*YEAR*

Telling the Time

```
M N C J A H T N K E P V P I K
E O P L V O Z E Y T M E K B R
T D R N U D M H N F I N I S H
U L P N M T E C N P G Y U U M
N K D A I K Z S R I A W G M S
I Z F F T N U S C D G S C S J
M E P I C N G Z D A Q H T J F
T V M E S M O I E U U O T L D
Y E Y E S K M O Z P A Z A O N
T N T Y L I D J N T R H J L O
N I A O N F R O G R T E F A C
E N V O D W S N R A E F O H E
W G O C L O C K U T R T O S S
T S E T A L F F Y S H U F J Z
S U V Y E A R L Y F R U M A V
```

What *TIME* is it?

....

It is *MIDDAY.*

....

It is … *O'CLOCK.*

....

MORNING

....

AFTERNOON

....

EVENING

....

NIGHT

....

SECOND

....

MINUTE

....

HOUR

....

EARLY

....

LATE

....

SOON

....

What time does it *START /*
FINISH?

....

TEN PAST

....

TWENTY past

....

QUARTER past

....

HALF past

....

SUNRISE

....

SUNSET

....

The Weather

```
L A Y A Y N J R R T W R Y L V
D Y F D N B N B S G J A R F N
D C N I D E J A R N V I R A W
T I A C E L C D M I L N H M E
W U O D G E Y S O W Z I Y R A
R L T H R S G S P O P N S H T
D E N O E D U G L N G G S A H
Y S F V E F A N N S F F U I E
N B T V S G E J H I C N M L R
N B O O M I S T Y A Z U B I D
U H H P R H Y C P B T E R N K
S K F S M M C L O U D Y E G H
M K G E C H Y W F O V E L R M
C T E M P E R A T U R E L T F
T A O C N I A R L U T K A K F
```

What is the *FORECAST*?	It is *COLD*.	It is *MISTY*.
What is the *TEMPERATURE*?	It is *SUNNY*.	It is *HAILING*.
It is … *DEGREES*.	It is *RAINING*.	It is *FREEZING*.
What is the *WEATHER* like?	It is *CLOUDY*.	Where can I buy a *RAINCOAT*?
It is *GOOD*.	It is *STORMY*.	Where can I buy an *UMBRELLA*?
It is *BAD*.	It is *WINDY*.	Where can I buy a *FAN*?
It is *WARM*.	It is *SNOWING*.	Where can I buy a *SUNHAT*?
It is *HOT*.	It is *ICY*.	

Common Verbs

```
U O M S S Z S M K V E D J R W
N F H M W R I T E B S U E B A
D G F T N K M J A E K A T N I
E S R Z K N C P G R D H P N T
R T K R H Z S H E Z T W O N K
S O O I Z A H C V S V E K A M
T W H I C W V R I T Z F F F C
A U R N S P U E G A O Z E W I
N H V S E K W E A Y C M E R W
D S G J F H X R B O P U L Z Y
K I H E E I D F M P L R B E E
D N D A S D Y E E N U E C W S
K I I T C L M E T S P E A K J
N F A R J O L D E E N R J V H
A G I U D S F B U Y V Y G Y E
```

To *EAT*

....

To *DRINK*

....

To *USE*

....

To *WORK*

....

To *HAVE*

....

To *COME*

....

To *NEED*

....

To *SPEAK*

....

To *GIVE*

....

To *KNOW*

....

To *LEAVE*

....

To *STAY*

....

To *SLEEP*

....

To *UNDERSTAND*

....

To *TAKE*

....

To *START*

....

To *FINISH*

....

To *WAIT*

....

To *EXIST*

....

To *BUY*

....

To *FEEL*

....

To *MAKE*

....

To *READ*

....

To *WRITE*

....

Stately Homes and Castles

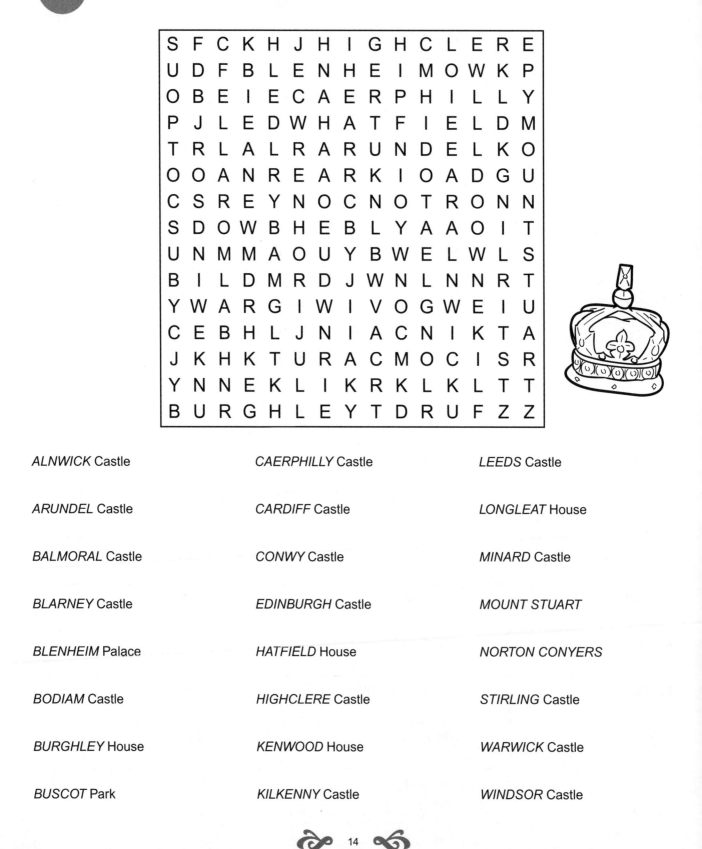

```
S F C K H J H I G H C L E R E
U D F B L E N H E I M O W K P
O B E I E C A E R P H I L L Y
P J L E D W H A T F I E L D M
T R L A R A R U N D E L K O
O O A N R E A R K I O A D G U
C S R E Y N O C N O T R O N N
S D O W B H E B L Y A A O I T
U N M M A O U Y B W E L W L S
B I L D M R D J W N L N N R T
Y W A R G I W I V O G W E I U
C E B H L J N I A C N I K T A
J K H K T U R A C M O C I S R
Y N N E K L I K R K L K L T T
B U R G H L E Y T D R U F Z Z
```

ALNWICK Castle	*CAERPHILLY* Castle	*LEEDS* Castle
ARUNDEL Castle	*CARDIFF* Castle	*LONGLEAT* House
BALMORAL Castle	*CONWY* Castle	*MINARD* Castle
BLARNEY Castle	*EDINBURGH* Castle	*MOUNT STUART*
BLENHEIM Palace	*HATFIELD* House	*NORTON CONYERS*
BODIAM Castle	*HIGHCLERE* Castle	*STIRLING* Castle
BURGHLEY House	*KENWOOD* House	*WARWICK* Castle
BUSCOT Park	*KILKENNY* Castle	*WINDSOR* Castle

Common Adjectives

```
T S S L A N T I W L D Y F O G
K Z L H L O O N S P A K J D N
Z D A O O A N K E I S O N C I
P E R C W R T S N I M N T P T
D S G O V P T E R I C P G A S
L O E L M F Y Y E M A N L T U
Y L Y D N E P O D Y B P A E G
P C W R P T T M O A K A R X S
P K D E R I T O M J W E J P I
A L G U F S T T O G F H B E D
H D E T A C I L P M O C U N U
V W W F V Y N R Y O B Y A S R
M V D E H S M A L L O E I I M
W G L P N O L F M J J R C V Y
Y L G U Y T T E R P W H F E I
```

PRETTY

UGLY

HAPPY

SAD

TALL

SHORT

LARGE

SMALL

SIMPLE

COMPLICATED

RICH

POOR

DISGUSTING

MODERN

ANCIENT

OPEN

CLOSED

TIRED

HOT

COLD

EXPENSIVE

CHEAP

FAST

SLOW

Prepositions

```
N Y E H S H E T T N O R F C C
P W K O U S S Z F A E Z M H O
J N S E U N F R E T F A O J T
C A G A I N S T O C G N R B P
Y Y C N G F S J S I N C E E E
B E J E O C O R N E R F D T C
B S W P R M W W Y M O I N W X
H U A E A E A K D R S O I E E
L S J D B R H G E N T T H E T
T P G I O B O W I T A T E N H
U E O S V J B U Y D R X B S R
G O N T E E I E N R T E F L O
U K M U L A W T N D E N K S U
O P P O S I T E F D O V O A G
Y C W C N M D N O Y E B E U H
```

ABOVE	At the *END* of	OUTSIDE
BELOW	BECAUSE of	NEAR
AFTER	BEHIND	NEXT TO
BEFORE	In *FRONT* of	On the *CORNER* of
AGAINST	EVERYWHERE	OPPOSITE
AMONG / BETWEEN	EXCEPT	PAST
AROUND	BEYOND	SINCE
At the *START* of	INSIDE	THROUGH

Adverbs

```
Y N Y J P T W O R R O M O T E
D E F R N T Y O O N S C Z S W
A V H V E L H R T S M O R E Y
O E O D K V E E L N S Z L L L
R R I C V S Y K N E D I S N I
B L I J J Y L L U F E R A C A
A U W V N B J O I C E V L L D
Q V Z O L E S S W P F R W J F
V Z O L C V U L G L P A E G E
E S W L N M O H K O Y A F H U
U R E A L L Y W J S L A H S T
M Y E S T E R D A Y T U D Z K
I W K H J W H E N N J T A O E
Y B L R W F V O B M A A P N T
K N Y U V L W O U T S I D E F
```

DAILY

....

WEEKLY

....

NEVER

....

ALWAYS

....

NOW

....

SOON

....

TODAY

....

TOMORROW

....

YESTERDAY

....

THEN

....

WHEN

....

QUICKLY

....

SLOWLY

....

HAPPILY

....

ABROAD

....

THERE

....

LESS

....

MORE

....

INSIDE

....

OUTSIDE

....

REALLY

....

VERY

....

WHERE

....

CAREFULLY

....

Travel

```
Y R O T S I H G R S T Z D L Y
Y E A E R U T A N B M S M E I
P E O P L E G J J Y L E R A R
M U Y L L A N O I S A C C O O
E K W N I A D E T I S I V N W
S E S L O C E R U T L U C B C
I T I Y C T G N Y O H Z E M U
J K G M Z I A O E V N S K B I
E I H M U V U F E X T G M C S
E K T J Y I G T G A T U D A I
O R S Y L T N E U Q E R F G N
H F E E B I A B A B O U T E E
Y P A H V E L E V A R T A I Z
C R P I W S E P Z U F O H Y A
N Z U C M K U N P O K W W C H
```

Do you *TRAVEL* often?

....

I travel *RARELY*.

....

I travel *OCCASIONALLY*.

....

I travel *FREQUENTLY*.

....

WHERE have you *VISITED*?

....

I have *BEEN* to …

....

Where is the *BEST* place you have been?

....

Where is the *WORST* place you have been?

....

WHAT do you *LIKE* to do when you travel?

....

I like to see the *SIGHTS*.

....

I like to *LEARN* about the *CULTURE*.

....

I like to learn *ABOUT* the *HISTORY*.

....

I like to try the local *CUISINE*.

....

I like to learn the *LANGUAGE*.

....

I like to meet the *PEOPLE*.

....

I like to see *NATURE*.

....

I like to do sporting *ACTIVITIES*.

....

Where would you like to visit *NEXT*?

....

Air Travel

```
B K T B T E R M I N A L L P B
F G E O S E R U T R A P E D J
E I K A Y H T Y M O N O C E D
E B N R T F N R T J B V C V F
R C S D N T T N O B W H G I R
F V H I A T I D K P E O R Z A
Y K T N D R I H E C S S Y B L
T I W G N W R C K K T S G W U
U W W M E I E I K J C S A K G
D F F C T A N F V E P E R P G
E C N A T S I S S A T N H M A
D P S F A L E T E W L I Z C G
R J U S C P E R I D R S M D E
B A G G A G E A E H N U S P P
T A E S N P C C S H L B U W P
```

Which *TERMINAL* do I need?	My seat is in *FIRST* class.	*DUTY FREE*.
Where do I *CHECK IN*?	Here is my *PASSPORT*.	*BAGGAGE* claim.
Where is the *ARRIVALS* hall?	Here is my *TICKET*.	Flight *ATTENDANT*.
Where is the *DEPARTURES* hall?	*HERE* is my boarding pass.	Where are the *CARTS*?
Where is the *BOARDING* gate?	Here is my *LUGGAGE*.	I cannot *FIND* my luggage.
My *SEAT* is in *ECONOMY*.	I do not have any *CHECKED* luggage.	I need *ASSISTANCE*.
My seat is in *BUSINESS* class.		

Getting Around

14

```
J C S D L V D A Y E B S B E U
T O B Z P K D E M F S J S N P
S Y F L R G J U Y A L K I B F
A R U V G I C G L A U I L N E
L O R B R H C J R L T G H U U
S S N W H E H W F Z H E A H L
V I R E T W M W E T G E D H T
I B B U W D E L R N C N E H W
U Z R G E A B P E A W H M I F
T N G I I A Y M H W P I U R F
E S A N T F K W G P B W L E O
K U K E O H I V K B H O P F T
C B M C C L W R O T G K O E E
I I R A K G V O S J M P V T G
T B Y R M S K C F T R A I N Z
```

One *TICKET*, please.

....

What time is the next *BUS*?

....

WHAT time is the train?

....

Can I *BOOK* a *FLIGHT*?

....

Can I *HIRE* a *CAR*?

....

Can you tell me *WHEN* we get to …?

....

What time is the *FIRST* bus?

....

What time is the *LAST* train?

....

How *LONG* will we be *DELAYED*?

....

I *WANT* to go to …

....

I would like to GET OFF at …

....

I want to get off *HERE*.

....

How *MUCH* is it?

....

Where can I *BUY* a ticket?

....

ONE-WAY ticket.

....

RETURN ticket.

....

First *CLASS* ticket.

....

Do you have a *TIMETABLE*?

....

Is this the *TRAIN* to …?

....

20

Border Crossing

```
Y C A L R P L E H L P A B R L
P G Y N E Y P L E A S E S D Y
U H N N A L T S I S S G K I S
T B P I A Y M K D Y W Y U K V
G C U N O O B L O R T N O C Y
Y N N S T G S J J E D K G F A
N E I S I T D L T E M N B L D
D Z U H A N H E R E I P A S I
G C D Y T R E S P H L I C Y L
K G I E T O T S T P C K E A O
Z N W N C A N E S I C O D D H
G C R S N L M I F M A A U T J
E T A D M O A F E N I M W H R
D P A S S P O R T I S B Z A Z
Y U D Y T I H Y E Y M L N T D
```

CUSTOMS

....

OFFICIAL

....

Passport CONTROL

....

I am here for … DAYS.

....

I do not have a PLANNED
departure DATE.

....

Your PASSPORT / visa PLEASE.

....

HERE is my passport / VISA.

....

I am GOING to …

....

I am here on BUSINESS.

....

I am here on HOLIDAY / vacation.

....

I am STAYING at …

....

I have NOTHING to DECLARE.

....

I have SOMETHING to declare.

....

THAT is mine.

....

That is not MINE.

....

I do not UNDERSTAND.

....

Can you HELP me?

....

Directions

```
D A G U T C L L Z C R O P K R
N B I L H T M T O Z A P C A N
I B A D I J L R O G E P F W L
H A E S S W N G N I N O L Z V
E W E J R E L E U C T S O T H
B A H Y R R E T V Y J I J T K
N Y B A E D J G S Y C T F E M
I L W O E M S W I O H E M A U
H E R E U C E N I G L I P F N
T I C F H T N S I Y N L R R E
I P L E H N R A U U H U I O X
W W S P S B R Y T C V Z G N T
U Y H I S T E E J S X O H T T
E W O T S G S G R U I E T F O
F R W J M D F R V B H D Z M Y
```

EXCUSE ME.

....

Can you *HELP* me?

....

I am *LOST.*

....

Is *THIS* the way to the …?

....

Is it *FAR*?

....

Is it *WITHIN* walking *DISTANCE*?

....

It is not far *AWAY.*

....

It is *ABOUT* 10 *MINUTES.*

....

You *NEED* to take a *BUS.*

....

Can you *SHOW* me (on the *MAP*)?

....

BEHIND …

....

HERE

....

In *FRONT* of …

....

LEFT

....

RIGHT

....

NEAR

....

NEXT TO …

....

OPPOSITE …

....

STRAIGHT ahead

....

CORNER

....

Car and Bike Rental

```
G K O E W J T L G L P U M P S
N H M E L W I K E G A E L I M
I A E E L C Y C R O T O M M S
N K P L E G Y F B C C S U I C
O E A N M J O C E K P C O G O
I H C U N E J R I J H B M C O
T E L O T W T G U B L L S Y T
I R T C D O O B K H D Y W L E
D T B A Z O M S V O A L B W R
N L A U N A M A J D L E I N R
O K Y O R V L D T A Y H O H Z
C D P J P W T E T I D P P R C
R M D E O V R N W C C W K K E
I D A A F I E C N A R U S N I
A H V C W R N A P R I L J I G
```

Where is the car *RENTAL* desk?

....

I want to rent a *CAR*.

....

I want to rent a *MOTORCYCLE*.

....

I want to rent a *BICYCLE*.

....

I would like to rent a *SCOOTER*.

....

For … *DAYS*.

....

For one *WEEK*.

....

I would like an *AUTOMATIC*.

....

I would like a *MANUAL* transmission.

....

Does it have *AIR CONDITIONING*?

....

How MUCH does it COST?

....

Does that include MILEAGE?

....

Does that include *INSURANCE*?

....

Here is my driver's *LICENCE /* license.

....

Do you have a cycle *HELMET*?

....

Do you have a *LOCK*?

....

Do you have a *PUMP*?

....

Do you have a *CHILD* seat?

....

23

Parts of a Car

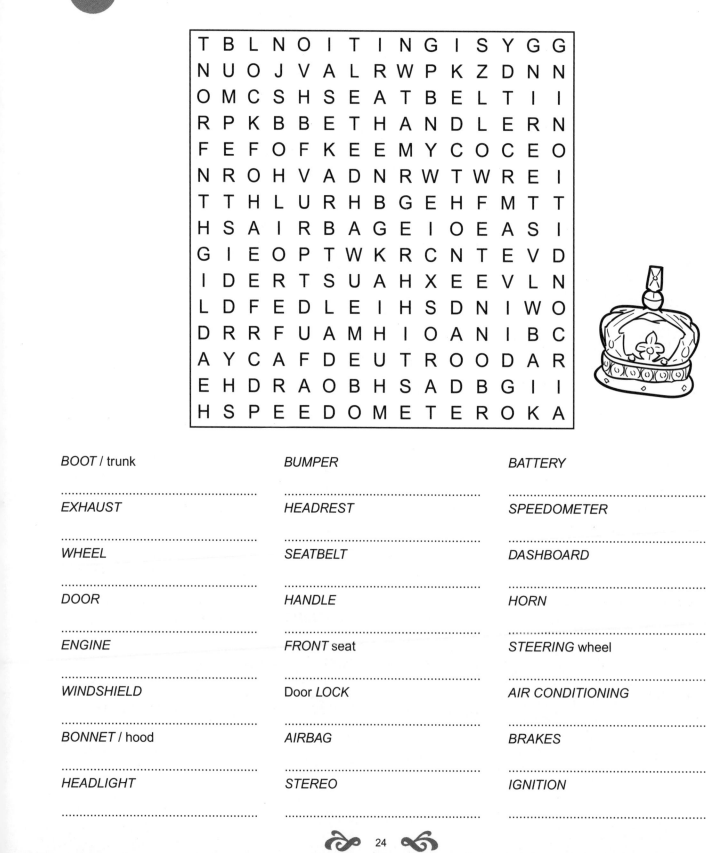

```
T B L N O I T I N G I S Y G G
N U O J V A L R W P K Z D N N
O M C S H S E A T B E L T I I
R P K B B E T H A N D L E R N
F E F O F K E E M Y C O C E O
N R O H V A D N R W T W R E I
T T H L U R H B G E H F M T T
H S A I R B A G E I O E A S I
G I E O P T W K R C N T E V D
I D E R T S U A H X E E V L N
L D F E D L E I H S D N I W O
D R R F U A M H I O A N I B C
A Y C A F D E U T R O O D A R
E H D R A O B H S A D B G I I
H S P E E D O M E T E R O K A
```

BOOT / trunk	*BUMPER*	*BATTERY*
EXHAUST	*HEADREST*	*SPEEDOMETER*
WHEEL	*SEATBELT*	*DASHBOARD*
DOOR	*HANDLE*	*HORN*
ENGINE	*FRONT* seat	*STEERING* wheel
WINDSHIELD	Door *LOCK*	*AIR CONDITIONING*
BONNET / hood	*AIRBAG*	*BRAKES*
HEADLIGHT	*STEREO*	*IGNITION*

Driving

```
H T V T N E D I C C A H R R V
R R N U C L A E S Z A E Z Y O
K O W N R E G A R A G F V A T
V R O O U J Y W I N M Z K W D
F M D E O P A H A E D W P E Y
J D N N T T Y D C R U Y Z N K
L S E T E K N H N E Y S T O P
Y L K R D C A N O H K Y I Y D
A O O Y V N N P P S T C M L F
W W R T I W A A A V P I E A R
E D B C S O I L R C T E X H A
V O E T W D A C K T B A E E C
I W E S C A S L I A N O N D J
G N B C J O D H N T A E Y E R
S C I T U R M P G T D A E J J
```

Is this the *ROAD* to …?	I have had an *ACCIDENT*.	*ONE WAY*
Where is the nearest *GARAGE*?	What is the *SPEED* limit?	*SLOW DOWN*
Can you *CHECK* the *OIL*?	*ENTRANCE*	*TOLL*
Can you check the *WATER* level?	*EXIT*	*DANGER*
Can I park *HERE*?	*NO PARKING*	*NO ENTRY*
I need a *MECHANIC*.	*GIVE WAY*	*STOP*
The car has *BROKEN DOWN*.	*DETOUR*	

Accommodation

```
B K Z S I N G L E L B T B O B
G E B L R L J Y L I M A F N R
Z E R S L E G B I K A F E W E
D W D L G U S R K U B A J E C
A U T B J G F E O V R N C L O
C F U O E U A A R B J I A B M
C J O S R E L K Y V L G M U M
E O K O M S H F N P A H P O E
S D C R O T R A J E B T S D N
S B E R I H W S F I A S I E D
I N H Y P O U T N F J C T O U
B A C O H U T C R R F L E F N
L J U V T S Y B R P I O A B H
E Y M U L E T S O H H T U O Y
G W Y U E S L F O A E P C M D
```

Can you tell me where there is a
BED and *BREAKFAST*?

....

Can you tell me where there is a
CAMPSITE?

....

Can you tell me where there is a
GUEST HOUSE?

....

Can you tell me where there is a
YOUTH HOSTEL?

....

Can you tell me where there is a
HOTEL?

....

Can you *RECOMMEND*
somewhere *NEARBY*?

....

Do you have a *SINGLE* room?

....

I would like a *DOUBLE* room.

....

Do you have an *ACCESSIBLE*
room?

....

Do you have a *FAMILY* room?

....

What time is *CHECKOUT*?

....

I have a *RESERVATION.*

....

I am *SORRY*, we are *FULL*.

....

For how many *NIGHTS*?

....

How *MUCH* is it per night?

....

How much is it per *WEEK*?

....

In the Hotel Room

```
R A N I T V Y Z T E A V J A D
E F G R E S T A U R A N T O M
T U S W I N F M O C E R U R Z
A U K O A H D L K I F B I B H
E F N F K B E L C Y L I M A F
H H K J T W P A E E E O B U L
B C B B E O L M H P C P R J N
M E K K L D D S C P L A E U L
K R D F E N C R E U M M Y N U
K P C D V I H O O L Y Z R V K
E I B E I W L S L W G T D F S
Y L I G S N E N D D S N R G S
T L L M I F G L U Y R S I I W
R O L B O F A I D D V L A S D
Z W H Z N D L K F P S T H P E
```

The room is too *HOT*.

....

The room is too *COLD*.

....

The room is too *NOISY*.

....

The room is too *SMALL*.

....

The room is *DIRTY*.

....

The *TELEVISION* does not work.

....

The *HEATER* does not work.

....

The *FAN* does not work.

....

The *WINDOW* does not open.

....

What is the Wi-Fi *PASSWORD*?

....

What time do I need to
   CHECK OUT?

....

May I have the *BILL*, please?

....

I would like a *SINGLE* room.

....

Do you have a *DOUBLE* room?

....

I would like a *FAMILY* room.

....

Is there a *RESTAURANT*?

....

Room *NUMBER*

....

KEY

....

HAIRDRYER

....

BEDDING

....

PILLOW

....

Camping

```
Y S M B L K P T L A U N D R Y
A H O W E R E G E S S Y A D E
T O H E I C A T K N T M S O L
S W W C P R G R L I T M M N O
H E E T B G A N C L S A O E O
T R D A P P G I S R V D O A P
B S G B H I R E E A H E R R G
W E J F F T C C K Z O T E N
H A L U C H Y A P M E A S S I
E K O E G C N W E Z V S E T M
R C L I L C H E O R S T R W M
E E N I I A L A G R O G A V I
C I N E O M C U R I R T A A W
W G S Z V P L R R G E O S B S
G D P E Y D L N F R E F B A H
```

WHERE is the *NEAREST* campsite?

....

Can we *CAMP* here?

....

Can I *PARK* next to my *TENT*?

....

Do you have any *VACANCIES*?

....

What is the *CHARGE* per *NIGHT*?

....

What is the charge per *WEEK*?

....

Does the *PRICE* include *ELECTRICITY*?

....

Does the price include hot *WATER*?

....

We want to *STAY* for ... *DAYS*.

....

Where are the *RESTROOMS*?

....

Where should I put my rubbish / *GARBAGE* / *RECYCLING*?

....

Are there *SHOWERS*?

....

Are there *LAUNDRY* facilities?

....

Are there tents for *HIRE*?

....

Is there a *STORE*?

....

Is there a *SWIMMING POOL*?

....

Could I *BORROW* a / an ...?

....

Shopping

```
O Y I G Y R G R C A S H H F J
I F A U L T Y V F H J D T W G
L B J C M D Z D F S S H E A R
K R B A R E C E I P T I S E N
I U J S U E E J Z L Z F G Y N
Y G V V R R D M E Y H N I U N
S N T V E W K I B B A R S G T
F I W H M F N S T H R U T W G
A H W G P G W I C C I T S B G
Y T K T D C F X I W A E W I N
O O C Y P C E J N W Y R R J I
H L B A E F W R A P P E D B K
O C Y N O N F Z H G E E H S O
N B U O B T O P U G B D N J O
O R D M K V U M T E L B F P L
```

WHERE is a …?

....

Where can I buy *GIFTS*?

....

Where can I buy *FOOD*?

....

Where can I buy *CLOTHING*?

....

How *MUCH* is this?

....

I would like to *BUY* …

....

I am just *LOOKING*.

....

Could I have a *BAG* please?

....

I do not *NEED* a *RECEIPT*, thank you.

....

Could I have it *WRAPPED*?

....

It is *FAULTY*.

....

Can I *PAY* with *CASH*?

....

Do you accept *CREDIT CARDS*?

....

I would like to *RETURN* it.

....

I would like my *MONEY* back, please.

....

I want to *EXCHANGE* this.

....

Stores and Amenities

K G A E R U T I N R U F V M H
W K T O B A C C O N I S T O R
Y T T K O M H L L Y W O T P E
R L L G N M I T O Y S H O P L
D E L I C A T E S S E N K G L
N D H P T R B O O K S T O R E
U S G O C K Z F R B B M P O S
A M Y H L E J R B R L H O C H
L C Y S O T A T F A A T A E S
W E A T T B R N R R O D E R I
V S V F H E M E M U Z Z T Y F
R H A I E U N A R B A K E R Y
S O L G S E C I F F O T S O P
W E N I G Y S B O U T I Q U E
C U C P E T S H O P B U T T Y
```

MARKET

FISH SELLER

BANK

POST OFFICE

GROCERY store

BAKERY

DELICATESSEN

BOOKSTORE

FURNITURE store

TOBACCONIST

SHOE store

BOUTIQUE

PHARMACY

TAILOR

GIFT SHOP

GENERAL store

CAFE

BAR

TOURIST information

LAUNDRY

PET SHOP

CLOTHES store

TOY SHOP

MUSIC shop
```

At the Hardware Store

```
S  C  V  R  Z  R  E  P  A  P  D  N  A  S  E
P  G  V  A  R  N  I  S  H  P  F  O  H  E  H
A  K  N  N  T  P  W  R  S  L  I  A  N  P
N  S  U  U  W  Y  A  S  E  U  S  X  H  Z
N  A  C  T  C  S  T  O  D  R  I  R  P  E  L
E  D  V  R  M  H  U  H  T  H  S  L  G  L  D
R  G  A  M  E  E  I  B  I  O  A  J  P  P  K
L  K  E  B  Z  W  T  S  A  N  O  R  Z  R  I
K  D  Z  T  B  F  D  I  E  M  G  L  S  G  Z
E  W  E  J  V  R  J  R  F  L  P  M  S  L  M
L  W  T  E  I  F  Z  F  I  R  E  M  M  A  H
I  O  M  L  N  G  D  V  N  V  Y  U  L  L  V
F  R  L  B  B  L  G  R  H  J  E  L  G  A  A
U  K  O  A  P  P  V  U  S  W  E  R  C  S  P
U  M  V  G  H  S  U  R  B  T  N  I  A  P  Y
```

TOOLS	MALLET	SCREWS
Have you got *ANYTHING* for …?	*SAW*	A pair of *PLIERS*
What would I need to *FIX* …?	*SPANNER*	*DRILL*
Can you *HELP* me?	*SCREWDRIVER*	*CHISEL*
That is just what I *NEED*.	*SANDPAPER*	*PLANE*
How does this *WORK*?	*FILE*	*PAINTBRUSH*
I need a *HAMMER*.	*NAILS*	*VARNISH*

Writers

```
E L V S P T N F H U R D A K J
C L Y U M D B A N F B B E K E
G O D S B S I V K B E A H N W
A R R N M N N O D J T W U I Z
I R A F A I W E R S A J G C Y
M A H H R M T D K U A M H J S
A C P T L I K H R C G R E Z N
N E F L O O W C P A I I S S R
Z M M E W L T E A S L D H O U
A J A A E G K S T L I L L S B
D Y W N U M I I I N B I A O I
A F F V T S E N E R O A W B W
M W I L D E T N T N A R P U R
S O R W E L L E V O R V B Z I
C M Y K E K V P N P U A E D T
```

Douglas *ADAMS*	Bernadine *EVARISTO*	Hilary *MANTEL*
Jane *AUSTEN*	Charles *DICKENS*	Christopher *MARLOWE*
J.G. *BALLARD*	Neil *GAIMAN*	George *ORWELL*
Malorie *BLACKMAN*	Thomas *HARDY*	Zadie *SMITH*
Charlotte *BRONTE*	Ted *HUGHES*	J.R.R. *TOLKIEN*
Robert *BURNS*	Kazuo *ISHIGURO*	Oscar *WILDE*
Lewis *CARROLL*	P.D. *JAMES*	Virginia *WOOLF*
Agatha *CHRISTIE*	John *KEATS*	Benjamin *ZEPHANIAH*

At the Hairdresser / Salon

```
H D T N Y L R U C J T N S N F
I H T R I M R T N R I H B T A
G A I C S U E I B I O U N T O
H I V P W L Y A A R W E O C D
L R S K S B I R T H M W L T L
I D B T D W P A D T Y V A W U
G R Z L V H R A N W E R R T E
H E T N E H A I R L O S D L M
T S B U B W O I T T W L Y O U
S S A P C P O T R O I T B D I
C E R G P R I T R D S N R O V
Z R B A J L I B N R R A G E O
D G E P I V E A I U E Y R I U
F N R A E Y A A H B J Y E M O
T O A P E I H G Y E N I F R N
```

HAIRDRYER

....

HAIRSTYLE

....

Hot *TOWEL*

....

HAIRDRESSER

....

BARBER

....

I want a side *PARTING*.

....

I would like *HIGHLIGHTS*.

....

I would like a *TRIM*.

....

I would like a *HAIRCUT*.

....

I would like a *BLOW DRY*.

....

I need a *BEARD* trim.

....

I have *CURLY* hair.

....

I have *FINE* hair.

....

I have *WAVY* hair.

....

I have *DRY HAIR*.

....

Can you do my *EYEBROWS*?

....

Can you do my *NAILS*?

....

How *SHORT* would you like it?

....

I would like it *VERY* short.

....

Just a *LITTLE* off.

....

I would like an *APPOINTMENT*,
    please.

....

Clothing

```
W S A V S B J B S H A W L C D
I R O N Y O P R K Y H T L F O
E I A C G O E G I P T E P Z O
T E D O K T S V R J H L S S H
J E I C A S M E T K S L C T R
J U O E G T F I V E B A J R A
B Z W O R A G O O U W C O E
S S S H I G H H E E L S A P W
H N H U U E S U C B D G R S R
O J R A I N C O A T T B D W E
R A A D N T T S E R F D I J D
T C R H R D C M I A W C G B N
S K I I S E B H R E R S A E U
W E C L Z J S A N T Y B N L P
S T A I J I Y S G S S K P T L
```

JEANS	RAINCOAT	HANDBAG
SHOES	SWEATER	HAT
HIGH HEELS	CARDIGAN	GLOVES
SPORTS shoes	HOOD	WALLET
BOOTS	SOCKS	SUIT
SKIRT	UNDERWEAR	SHIRT
DRESS	BRA	SHORTS
JACKET	BELT	SHAWL

Communications

```
S R R S H N C P M O T R K E I
S M A R T P H O N E F Y W P S
E A F T Y A V D R A C T S O P
R R J E E D M Z W O O O R L E
D L T N O K G P N O C A A E A
D B F R J H S N S I T S I V K
A N B E O V E U A N E Z Y N I
K L A T S C M L P U U M V E N
R E U N T U M A L O Y M A K G
E D W I O E N U I O T P B I U
I J O W D W T R N L J P A E L
R N A I R M A I L S B I A Z R
U J A I E T I S B E W O M L H
O P A C K A G E T H N J X M Z
C F R L E T C A T N O C G I U
```

I would like to buy some *STAMPS*, please.

....

I would like to send this *AIRMAIL*.

....

I need an *ENVELOPE*.

....

I would like a *POSTCARD*.

....

PACKAGE

....

COURIER

....

MAILBOX

....

Who is *SPEAKING*?

....

HELLO, this is …

....

I would like to *TALK* to …

....

SMARTPHONE

....

LAPTOP

....

INTERNET

....

EMAIL

....

WEBSITE

....

SOCIAL MEDIA

....

What is your phone *NUMBER*?

....

What is your email *ADDRESS*?

....

You can *CONTACT* me on / at …

....

There is a bad *CONNECTION*.

....

Money and Banking

```
Y G L T R E F S N A R T J L H
J U L W R J G N G I E R O F S
T T N U O C C A I V I E L I M
A D O C H A N G E V O E G O A
V E T A D J H E G I E N T S L
Z K E G C C T H P L T T M F L
Z N O R G F O R G O T T E N W
L E S O L C O C W L H W T Y M
O G R H V R H S A C A C I E S
V O G E A R R A N G E R L N E
Z M C T M O N E Y P D B G R F
T T S E R A E N I R O M C E W
K J G K B F N N A R I K G Y U
J L B S N I O C P J H G G J E
N O I T A C I F I T N E D I W
```

I would like to *ARRANGE* a *TRANSFER*.

....

I would like to get *CASH*.

....

I would like to exchange *MONEY*.

....

I would like to get *CHANGE* for this *NOTE*.

....

My *NAME* is …

....

When does the bank *CLOSE / OPEN*?

....

Where is the *NEAREST* ATM?

....

There is a *PROBLEM* with your *ACCOUNT*.

....

Can I see your *IDENTIFICATION*, please?

....

Please *SIGN* here.

....

Where is the *FOREIGN* exchange?

....

I have *FORGOTTEN* my *PIN*.

....

The ATM took my *CARD*.

....

I need *SMALL* change.

....

I need *LARGE* notes.

....

I need *COINS*.

....

Business

```
P D D K O F G U E W S B R N M
T D D T C N O N P E H D I T S
U U T U I Y O S W S S R A I V
J A V T K H B E K E P F F M M
U H E N P T B U U A A K E E T
A E A E O S Y G S E I N D G N
M H L B I U A H C I O S A T E
T E B T T E C N E L N M R B M
T M E S L U E O A V T E T T T
I S F L E R P S U R M H S P N
C B O I E M A D D R E S S S I
A C C F E S I S B P S O N O O
R P N P S H R N C H B E N R P
D O J C L A E M A M G D L Y P
C V E R Y W E L L R U B R U A
```

I am attending a *CONFERENCE*.

I am *ALONE*.

Here is my *WEBSITE*.

I am attending a *COURSE*.

I have an *APPOINTMENT* with …

That went *VERY WELL*.

I am going to a *MEETING*.

Do you have a *BUSINESS* card?

THANK YOU for your *TIME*.

I am visiting a *TRADE FAIR*.

Here is my business *CARD*.

Shall we go for a *MEAL*?

I am attending a *SEMINAR*.

Here is my *TELEPHONE* number.

I am with my *COLLEAGUES*.

Here is my email *ADDRESS*.

Tourist Attractions – London

```
E T R G Y E T R A F A L G A R
F N V A M E E L C U T B K T S
D E A A B T L F O N R R S A Z
B M D P A B H B E H A E H T A
H A H T I R E V M S O G T F F
M I K K E U O Y Y E P D E F B
S L F Y U C G T C B W I P I M
B R E G E N T L N I U R G G D
E A J S L U A P T S P B Y Y L
L P D Z C N G H Y D E M H H O
F B F E O L R Z D N I J Y L N
A L W I O E O T C M J N W L D
S Y T B W S K Y G A R D E N O
T A E O A V W S H A R D K S N
N O T P M A H W A R R O O M S
```

BIG BEN	KEW Gardens	ST. PAUL'S Cathedral
Churchill WAR ROOMS	LONDON Dungeon	TATE Modern
COVENT Garden	London EYE	The SHARD
CUTTY SARK	MADAME Tussauds	Tower BRIDGE
HAMPTON Court Palace	NATIONAL Gallery	TOWER of London
HMS BELFAST	OLYMPIC Park	TRAFALGAR Square
Houses of PARLIAMENT	SKY GARDEN	WEMBLEY Stadium
HYDE Park	Shakespeare's GLOBE	Westminster ABBEY

Occupations

```
E A B R E B M U L P K C A S U
G H U R E Y W A L S I S A T N
D E I L C S S R O M S L O I U
U D L I A V E L K I E C O W R
J I D B U T D J S S Z H T S
T T E R I I N T P C D U T E E
E O R A E E A E I D P W N R F
A R W R U N R E E A A M A E U
C M E I T S N N I I D U T M B
H I H A O T G N T R O S N R Z
E O W N I I T R E Y C I U A T
R E L S N E E K K W T C O F O
L F T E R S N Z H I O I C F B
W D E H S A Y C H D R A C G Y
L R M R B R E T I R W N A S T
```

Shop ASSISTANT	DOCTOR	LIBRARIAN
SALESPERSON	BANKER	JUDGE
NURSE	BUILDER	PAINTER
WAITRESS	CHEF	WRITER
WAITER	SCIENTIST	EDITOR
PLUMBER	ENGINEER	MUSICIAN
ACCOUNTANT	FARMER	PILOT
TEACHER	LAWYER	SOLDIER

In the Office

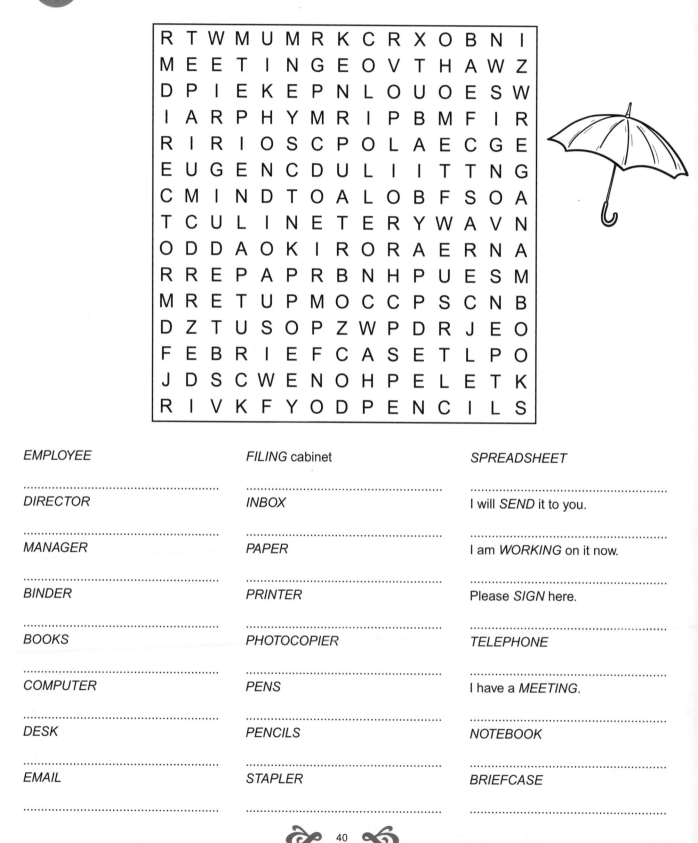

```
R T W M U M R K C R X O B N I
M E E T I N G E O V T H A W Z
D P I E K E P N L O U O E S W
I A R P H Y M R I P B M F I R
R I R I O S C P O L A E C G E
E U G E N C D U L I I T N G
C M I N D T O A L O B F S O A
T C U L I N E T E R Y W A V N
O D D A O K I R O R A E R N A
R R E P A P R B N H P U E S M
M R E T U P M O C C P S C N B
D Z T U S O P Z W P D R J E O
F E B R I E F C A S E T L P O
J D S C W E N O H P E L E T K
R I V K F Y O D P E N C I L S
```

EMPLOYEE	FILING cabinet	SPREADSHEET
DIRECTOR	INBOX	I will SEND it to you.
MANAGER	PAPER	I am WORKING on it now.
BINDER	PRINTER	Please SIGN here.
BOOKS	PHOTOCOPIER	TELEPHONE
COMPUTER	PENS	I have a MEETING.
DESK	PENCILS	NOTEBOOK
EMAIL	STAPLER	BRIEFCASE

Technology

```
R E T U P M O C M N M Z J P G
U S E R N A M E G A P E M O H
A P P L I C A T I O N L C T A
A H D Y U W P Z R E G D P P T
I A R V I K T O U S R R T A T
Y R O M E M S O P A O N N L A
B D W G M R C C O G U E I Z C
F D S N U W W B R O E N O E H
O R S C U R Y A C R T C S I M
L I A V S E M C C E P U U W E
D V P H K F A S R T O B P T N
E E A J H B I N G M N C L L T
R R M M S U E L D J B L O G G
E S A B A T A D E H C R A E S
I R E G I S T E R E K A D R O
```

ACCOUNT	FOLDER	PASSWORD
APPLICATION	HARD DRIVE	PROGRAM
ATTACHMENT	HOMEPAGE	To REGISTER
BLOG	INTERNET	SCREEN
COMPUTER	KEYBOARD	SEARCH engine
CURSOR	LAPTOP	To SHARE
DATABASE	MEMORY	To UPLOAD
FILE	MOUSE	USERNAME

Tourist Attractions – Outside London

```
H A D R I A N S T K T L S H A
L I L B P I T T R D O U W L G
O C O A R W E O A C K Z B L J
G H O N C I Y W H O S E E S E
S E P E P M G N I N R N I T F
K D K E Z H E H O T F E W O T
A D C D K S P W T I H A S N F
R A A L S R D N N O R A E E Y
A R L E B O I N R W N C I H Y
B Z B S N I A K I E U Y D E N
R F O A W N G C L L T R R N A
A E O O T I K P N A O N G G N
E D D S D H J U I F F U I E G
A Y P E N E D W X T U J Z T E
B E I S N E K O T S R E V A L
```

ALBERT Docks	DUNLUCE Castle	PITT Rivers Museum
ANGEL of the North	EDEN Project	SKARA BRAE
BATH	FALKIRK Wheel	SNOWDON
BIG PIT	GLENFINNAN Viaduct	STONEHENGE
BLACKPOOL Tower	HADRIAN'S Wall	The NEEDLES
BRIGHTON Pier	LAVERSTOKE Mill	TINTERN Abbey
CHEDDAR Gorge	LOCH NESS	WARWICK Castle
Chester ZOO	OXFORD	YORK Minster

Working Life

```
C B J V E J R V K D K A D B Y
E O R A A J S D O R R F R A R
G K M H Z S V N M B U S W A Y
N L N M W Y O J N E D G P Y D
T D L D U T H R E O N K J A T
B U E T J T B A N O J E U H S
L N F I U Y E E L V E R Y S U
F E S U T H M D I S T E Z R G
R P R B T I R L A P O H J A L
O E O E D R M S M A Z T T E Z
D J H D H B A E A K U W R Y I
B L E T Y W W V K L A W A M P
Z I F J O H Z M E B C O I W O
N K R A F Y R E V L S R N I R
I E U I I B C Y C L E K P J E
```

WHERE do you work?

....

I WORK at …

....

What is your JOB?

....

I AM A …

....

Do you have to COMMUTE?

....

I commute a LONG WAY.

....

I do not commute VERY FAR.

....

How do you TRAVEL to work?

....

I WALK.

....

I CYCLE.

....

I catch the BUS.

....

I catch the TRAIN.

....

Do you ENJOY your work?

....

I LIKE it / I DO NOT like it.

....

How long have you worked THERE?

....

For … YEARS.

....

A long TIME.

....

Not VERY long.

....

What OTHER jobs have you DONE?

....

I have ALSO worked as …

....

School Subjects and Activities

```
D K R E C N E I C S M H U K S
R G Y M N A S T I C S C G N C
A S P I G R U R U Z S N E H I
M Z D H S I N A P S E E O N T
A I H E N G L I S H H R G A A
T G L Z Y E I S Y C F R I M
P E T I E W C R G C D J A L E
R R C R T Y R O T S I H P A H
T M N H I E L C N S D S H T T
C A P B N O R M O O I I Y I A
S N C M I O H A U O M M U H M
L U L B R A L C T S K I E R P
Y G O L O I C O S U I E C H H
J C C M R H F J G Z R C R S C
N E C M M E D I A Y Z E K Y A
```

ART	TECHNOLOGY	CHOIR
HISTORY	DRAMA	MUSIC club
GEOGRAPHY	ENGLISH	CHESS club
MATHEMATICS	FRENCH	GYMNASTICS
PHYSICS	GERMAN	COOKERY
BIOLOGY	SPANISH	ECONOMICS
CHEMISTRY	ITALIAN	SOCIOLOGY
SCIENCE	MEDIA studies	LITERATURE

In the Classroom

```
W Q U E S U R Q U E S T I O N
V H G F L T N E M I R E P X E
N O I T A L S N A R T U N P P
L R B T P R A K R D K I L P T
R E E O E F E W G H I G C E V
K T S T H B J W L A R N H N R
S U R S N I O A S A V O G C Y
A P U B O E S A M N M U T I D
T M O O V N D M R E A N E L R
S O C J K K A U W D I Z A Z A
K C I Y H R B O T A E R C S W
R E P A P T R O P S N Y H R I
G D E S K K U R D L J F E G N
R B C S N O I T A U Q E R N G
U C M E R O T A L U C L A C C
```

QUESTION	LESSON	EXPERIMENT
ANSWER	TEACHER	PENCIL
TASK	ESSAY	PAPER
WHITEBOARD	DESK	BOOK
COMPUTER	COURSE	READING
CALCULATOR	PAINT	TRANSLATION
RULER	DRAWING	HOMEWORK
STUDENT	EQUATIONS	GRAMMAR

Colours / Colors

```
V J V A D B T K E T I H W P C
T Y K E E V N E Z T P V M R S
O Y R I Z I O Y D G N E E R G
C P G E P K R I L U L A O C S
I E P G O Z F B O H M E S W C
R L B N Y N F R G V I L D O Z
P R V A P R A O G O A P E L H
A E U R I M S N S T S R S L T
B V S O G A C Z Z C C U I E U
Y L B J R R B E A M A P O Y N
C I C B I N M R W O L W U K T
Z S H M W O L A B L I B Q C S
F D S O K E O M U I L D R A E
C O R Y T E P C D V V O U L H
N B A B L U E B A E E T T B C
```

APRICOT	CRIMSON	PURPLE
BEIGE	GOLD	RED
BLACK	GREEN	SAFFRON
BLUE	LILAC	SCARLET
BRONZE	MAUVE	SILVER
BROWN	OLIVE	TURQUOISE
CHESTNUT	ORANGE	WHITE
CREAM	PINK	YELLOW

Sightseeing

```
L N N W T E S O I D U A L O V
D O W F P S C K J R J R U G F
N S C U K J H Y R E L L A G V
G I M A L A C I R O T S I H M
L U L U L R D O F Y D C B S D
S U I R S K R D U H R O I H I
E K Z D I E O S E H A G C P S
T P N S E L U G Y T H L D A C
R A B T D B R M T T R U T R O
V H H E N A O R S N F U R G U
Y Z R T H G I O L W E Y O O N
C N T C T P J I K C S E U T T
G E D A Y T R I P K O B N O Z
O P S P O F K P L J L G U H A
I O N W Z F S N V P C F K P G
```

I would like an *AUDIO SET*.

....

I would like a *GUIDEBOOK*.

....

I would like a *LOCAL* map.

....

I would like to visit a *MUSEUM*.

....

I would like to go to a *GALLERY*.

....

Do you have information on local *SIGHTS*?

....

Do you have information on *HISTORICAL* sights?

....

Can I take *PHOTOGRAPHS*?

....

What is *THAT*?

....

What time does it *OPEN*?

....

What time does it *CLOSE*?

....

What is the admission *CHARGE*?

....

Is there a *DISCOUNT* for …?

....

Is there a discount for *OLDER* people?

....

When is the next *BOAT TRIP*?

....

When is the next *DAY TRIP*?

....

When is the next *TOUR*?

....

Buildings

```
S C N E R C I N E M A K B A F
K H O R W M P B I O Z J M D A
Y R I I T V U Z L A O N M N C
S D T F P R U E M O R U M E T
C W A R E H O U S E O T H S O
R E T E F L S P G U S H O O R
A Y S P G S A Y R N M P C E Y
P Y S U E A C R A I F Y T S L
E G U S O P R H D V A O P F E
R P B M A H T A U E H O W I K
W V R P P B N W G R H O N M Z
A G Y N N K M W N S C T T U W
O F F I C E Y E O I A H A E M
A D F K H O S P I T A L I C L
Y E C I L O P I E Y J C B G J
```

HOTEL	SCHOOL	AIRPORT
SHOP	CHURCH	SKYSCRAPER
WAREHOUSE	EMBASSY	GARAGE
FACTORY	FIRE station	CINEMA / movie theater
OFFICE building	POLICE station	TRAIN station
UNIVERSITY	POST office	BUS STATION
MUSEUM	TOWNHOUSE	HOSPITAL
	CATHEDRAL	

Places of Interest

```
A L A C I R O T S I H W M M M
B O L R S C A S I N O K L J U
J R L S E T N E M E S U M A S
B P A E P P A R H E W V O R E
R B F A A F O D E C P A K Z U
I G R A Y Z D M I V R K E N M
D K E R P I V D D U I U Z Q E
G S T T N E M U N O M R H U G
E N A G G E F I L D L I W C A
L I W A K L O O I D Y S H I L
P U B L M T M T R E C N O C L
M R E L R S Z J D B R F V C I
E R A E E A U O T S A O C F V
T J C R A C F T O W N H A L L
C I H Y N I G H T C L U B Y A
```

TOWN HALL	CASTLE	RIVER
BRIDGE	NIGHTCLUB	ZOO
MUSEUM	BEACH	HISTORICAL site
ART GALLERY	PARK	WILDLIFE sanctuary
MONUMENT	COAST	STADIUM
CHURCH	WATERFALL	AMUSEMENT park
TEMPLE	CONCERT hall	OPERA house
VILLAGE	RUINS	CASINO

```
V S S A T R A C A N G A M N E
H A S T I N G S Z O T D E T L
W C N A V M R P H L O Y X D I
O I O E D H Z I Z M C C H L Z
C D I R A S W P E A N S I R A
Y U N G P I E S M I W R B O B
T O U F N N D E N A S M I W E
A B B P G A R V L O A S T V T
E B L L Y P E N G S I T I N H
R O I A U S R M E T C I O O A
T S Y S C O A S I O R T N R N
H F E A C K O L Z R V A Z M A
I I I V D R A W D E C N G A J
D V U O G E N A M O R I F N R
L O N D O N V Z C G O C A A F
```

Acts of *SUPREMACY*	*ENGLISH* Civil War	*RMS TITANIC*
Battle of *HASTINGS*	Great *EXHIBITION*	Sealing of the *MAGNA CARTA*
BLACK Death	Great Fire of *LONDON*	*SPANISH* Armada defeated
BOUDICA'S rebellion	*GREAT* Reform Act	The Act of *UNION*
CRIMEAN war	Gunpowder *PLOT*	*TREATY* of Versailles
DOMESDAY Book	*NORMAN* Conquest	*V-E DAY*
EDWARD VIII abdicates	Repeal of the *CORN LAWS*	Wars of the *ROSES*
ELIZABETHAN era	*ROMAN* Invasion	*WORLD* Wars

45

At the Museum / Gallery

```
C S I Y G N O I S S I M D A K
E C N A S S I A N E R U R O I
W K N I E C I H P A R G S M B
G U O E J E V I S S E R P M I
L N I O A U D I O N E R D P S
A R T I B A J C U A E A M H D
U W I N M E Z W L S O B U O N
S V B A R B D L S D E L V T I
U P I F H U Y I E A B A D O M
N I H T J C O U U J O M I G E
U F X L S N L T F G O A Z R R
P D E U I I I E H D S P N A B
O F W S Z F T W E N G B E P T
H G M P U S H R N H L B P H H
V P Z L A G N V A S W V O S P
```

When is the museum *OPEN*?

....

How much is *ADMISSION*?

....

What is in the *EXHIBITION*?

....

I like *GRAPHIC* art.

....

I like *IMPRESSIONISM*.

....

I like *MODERN* art.

....

I like *RENAISSANCE* paintings.

....

Is there *WHEELCHAIR* access?

....

Can you tell me about the *ARTIST*?

....

How *OLD* is it?

....

I would *REALLY* like to *SEE* …

....

It *REMINDS* me of …

....

Is there a *TOUR*?

....

Can I take *PHOTOGRAPHS*?

....

It is *BEAUTIFUL*.

....

It is *UNUSUAL*.

....

It is *IMPRESSIVE*.

....

Is there an *AUDIO* guide?

....

Is there a *GUIDEBOOK*?

....

At the Beach

```
B T S E B I I E H W B E F N U
C H A I R R R D T S I S D S W
H U Y S G E G B P N K E Y I E
J O A C H V W T E D I N Q N T
S F T W C N R A P U N U O B S
E T J Y N R R E M J I S L E U
S C R A A E T B M E W I Z A I
S L O O S Z R I T I F C Z C T
A O F T N E M E M E C O B H J
L S L L G S M G D K P T B T
G E J L B T I U T O W E L A N
N D A G N N A J P A Z Y H L T
U F E Z G R H O O H W N O L W
S O M C D U L U V I U Z R C B
H P C S K G S U N S C R E E N
```

WHERE is the beach?	*STRONG* currents	*DECK* chair
Where is the *BEST* beach?	Beach *CLOSED*	*BEACHBALL*
Where is the *NEAREST* beach?	What time is high / low *TIDE*?	*SUNGLASSES*
Where is the *QUIETEST* beach?	Can I rent a *CHAIR*?	*BIKINI*
Is it *SAFE* to swim?	Can I rent an *UMBRELLA*?	*SUN HAT*
Is there a *LIFEGUARD*?	Can I rent a *WETSUIT*?	*SUNSCREEN*
NO SWIMMING	Beach *TOWEL*	

Travel with Children

```
P F U B R B B S U H B P C W M
D C O D O B I R M D W H H I U
K O U R A E R M E B I I H P D
R R O B M B C C G L D H F E G
Z A Y F F U W H D N L J C S G
S B R H K K L V F E M O T E D
B D E W O L L A U P P D R A I
H D E E F T S A E R B O A T H
V T T H A V M O P I Z P T D S
M E N U M M W F R U Z K B T O
E G F G I H I G H C H A I R Y
L Y Y I L C E W G D H U U D L
I L G K Y E L B A T I U S K I
V Y E A R O L D R E J U N T S
D O K S I E N A Z F Y P V V D
```

I need a baby / child *SEAT*.

....

I need a *POTTY*.

....

I need a *CRIB*.

....

I need a *STROLLER*.

....

I need a *HIGH CHAIR*.

....

Are children *ALLOWED*?

....

Is there a *BABY* change room?

....

Is there a *CHILD* discount?

....

Is there a *FAMILY* discount?

....

Is there a children's *MENU*?

....

Can I *BREASTFEED* here?

....

Do you sell *FORMULA*?

....

Do you *SELL* baby *FOOD*?

....

Do you sell baby *WIPES*?

....

Is it *SUITABLE* for ...-*YEAR-OLD*
children?

....

Disabled and Assisted Travel

```
L A K L E Y I I V U H M F S F
K E D S M N G K C I T S E S P
Y C L P I C T V H M T N G P Z
D T U B M E W R O F O R U E A
Z D I G I A N O A T M L I T P
D N I L B S R Z S N I A D S R
P L E H I H S E N A C D E A I
V S E U T B L E R F A E D S A
S M T A J B A D C L B C O E H
F E B A B E N S C C Z E G H C
R F F O I A D J I J A R S C L
A Z C Z H R B A G D E A I T E
M I I N K B S Y B S J R C U E
E C N A T S I S S A T R W R H
Z D E L B A S I D V P J O C W
```

I have a *DISABILITY*.

I am *DISABLED*.

WHEELCHAIR

Walking *STICK*

Walking *FRAME*

CRUTCHES

I am *BLIND*.

I am *DEAF*.

The *RAMP*

The *STEPS / STAIRS*

The *COBBLESTONES*

HANDRAIL

Is there a disabled *BATHROOM*?

Is there an *ENTRANCE* without steps?

Can you *HELP* me?

I require *ASSISTANCE*.

I need an *ACCESSIBLE* room.

Are *GUIDE DOGS* permitted?

Scientists

```
E R Z L L F C S C E W S M R U
G B R L O U R N G I P S N G C
I C H Z V Y R A E L I S T E R
N Y M P E G B T N R Z V J E V
T L U L L B N N C K A O J N F
V J L Z A E F I O R L L R O A
Y A L B C E A N K T I I C S R
H E F L E M I N G W R C N M A
Y T K F A W D S R K A Y K O D
X D H A R D G B I Z V H A H A
O A J A E G O C S A P O T T Y
C L D J I L H O D G K I N S Z
W T J H K Y I Z G T U R I N G
G O R D O N P R I E S T L E Y
C N L O M D P S P N E W T O N
```

Hertha *AYRTON*	Alexander *FLEMING*	Mary *LEAKEY*
Charles *BABBAGE*	Rosalind *FRANKLIN*	Joseph *LISTER*
Brian *COX*	Jane *GOODALL*	Ada *LOVELACE*
Francis *CRICK*	Isabella *GORDON*	Anne *MCLAREN*
John *DALTON*	Edmond *HALLEY*	Isaac *NEWTON*
Charles *DARWIN*	Stephen *HAWKING*	Joseph *PRIESTLEY*
Humphry *DAVY*	Peter *HIGGS*	William *THOMSON*
Michael *FARADAY*	Dorothy *HODGKIN*	Alan *TURING*

Sporting Stars

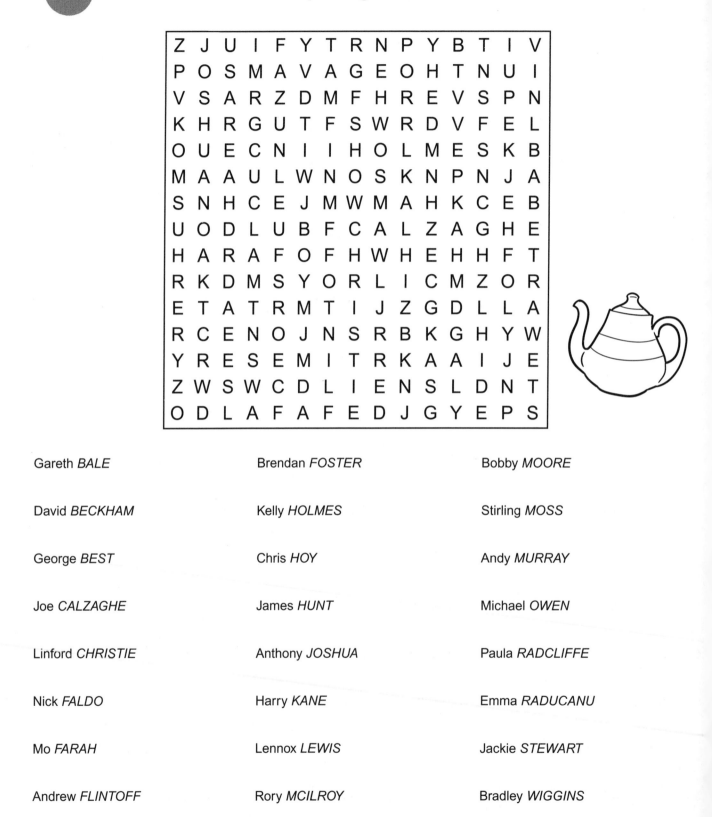

```
Z J U I F Y T R N P Y B T I V
P O S M A V A G E O H T N U I
V S A R Z D M F H R E V S P N
K H R G U T F S W R D V F E L
O U E C N I I H O L M E S K B
M A A U L W N O S K N P N J A
S N H C E J M W M A H K C E B
U O D L U B F C A L Z A G H E
H A R A F O F H W H E H H F T
R K D M S Y O R L I C M Z O R
E T A T R M T I J Z G D L L A
R C E N O J N S R B K G H Y W
Y R E S E M I T R K A A I J E
Z W S W C D L I E N S L D N T
O D L A F A F E D J G Y E P S
```

Gareth *BALE*	Brendan *FOSTER*	Bobby *MOORE*
David *BECKHAM*	Kelly *HOLMES*	Stirling *MOSS*
George *BEST*	Chris *HOY*	Andy *MURRAY*
Joe *CALZAGHE*	James *HUNT*	Michael *OWEN*
Linford *CHRISTIE*	Anthony *JOSHUA*	Paula *RADCLIFFE*
Nick *FALDO*	Harry *KANE*	Emma *RADUCANU*
Mo *FARAH*	Lennox *LEWIS*	Jackie *STEWART*
Andrew *FLINTOFF*	Rory *MCILROY*	Bradley *WIGGINS*

Meeting People – Conversation

```
N S R Y C I T S A T N A F P K
O E R V F B G N O L W O H N D
I K O U D K C U R R E N T L Y
T S Z S E L F E M P L O Y E D
A T O T R F E D R O P F K W L
C U R A I R R V W Y G N I O D
A D M E T V V A I L M A N Y P
V Y F R E T O H E L J J T K V
C O N G R A T U L A T I O N S
J W K G O C C H T E N K U H E
N V O E O I D I A R R B C V E
O U R R B A N K H O J E H Y Z
I E N W Y G J G W I R E N A D
H A P S S S E N I S U B E V W
U T C I N T E R E S T I N G S
```

Do you *LIVE* here?	I am here to *STUDY*.	How *INTERESTING*.
....	....	....
What are you *DOING*?	*HOW LONG* are you here?	*WHAT* do you do?
....	....	....
Where are you *GOING*?	I am here for … *DAYS*.	I *WORK* in …
....	....	....
Are you here on holiday / *VACATION*?	*GREAT!*	I am *SELF-EMPLOYED*.
....	....	....
I am *HERE* for a holiday / vacation.	*REALLY*?	I am *RETIRED*.
....	....	....
I am here for *BUSINESS*.	*CONGRATULATIONS!*	I am *CURRENTLY* studying.
....	....	....
	That is *FANTASTIC*.	Keep *IN TOUCH*!
	....	....

Family

```
C F O C A V Z D N A B S U H V
H R D U N C L E E D R I B L W
I J D C J U E P P A R T N E R
L R R E H T O M H U N S A F A
D R E H T A F D E G D Y O L M
R Y Y L H P E G W H Z P H N B
E E M U A R O Y Y T C W I F R
N V S B E T Y D W E V E U E O
G D I T K Z I I A R C Y T A T
H F S J H O F V B E T S B A H
J O I S S E D S E N I N M E E
F F H O R N C O U S I N U S R
Z T T F M N I S J R P V W A D
Z E U F B E L W T U O B A W E
T R E C U D O R T N I E E Z S
```

THIS IS MY …	BROTHER	UNCLE
……………………………	…………………………	…………………………
I would like to *INTRODUCE* you to my …	SISTER	NEPHEW
……………………………	…………………………	…………………………
Tell me *ABOUT* your …	HUSBAND	NIECE
……………………………	…………………………	…………………………
FATHER	WIFE	TWINS
……………………………	…………………………	…………………………
MOTHER	PARTNER	ADOPTED
……………………………	…………………………	…………………………
SON	CHILDREN	FOSTERED
……………………………	…………………………	…………………………
DAUGHTER	COUSIN	RELATIVES
……………………………	…………………………	…………………………
	AUNT	
	…………………………	

53 · Where Are You From?

```
S  J  N  A  K  T  I  E  R  T  U  D  T  S  C
R  U  R  A  L  A  R  E  A  S  Y  L  I  U  B
O  B  H  C  M  M  D  H  Z  R  V  E  L  H  E
M  W  I  F  Y  V  M  E  T  O  V  T  L  L  S
U  T  R  V  A  U  U  N  F  W  U  M  E  J  T
Y  O  B  M  O  S  U  C  S  R  T  O  W  N  L
M  V  P  I  M  O  W  M  E  B  V  U  S  Z  P
R  D  W  E  C  K  A  N  M  E  K  I  L  L  E
D  P  D  R  D  L  O  T  I  S  I  V  A  G  P
Z  T  Z  E  L  K  M  K  L  D  I  C  A  Z  D
D  D  L  H  D  Y  Z  O  T  B  E  L  U  L  R
J  S  M  W  E  D  J  A  K  V  L  E  O  D  J
E  W  E  T  V  N  R  Y  L  I  C  C  I  J  T
Z  U  C  I  I  J  H  Y  V  U  H  T  H  O  S
S  J  J  C  L  I  M  A  T  E  C  R  H  E  D
```

I AM FROM …

....

WHERE are you from?

....

What is the *BEST* thing about your *CULTURE*?

....

What is the *WORST* thing about where you are from?

....

Where should I *VISIT* in …?

....

Is it a big *COUNTRY*?

....

No, it is quite *SMALL.*

....

What is the *CLIMATE* like there?

....

HOT

....

COLD

....

WET

....

DRY

....

Have you *LIVED* anywhere *ELSE*?

....

Where was the best *PLACE* that you lived?

....

Do you live in a *CITY*?

....

Do you live in a *RURAL AREA*?

....

Do you live in a *TOWN*?

....

Do you live in a *VILLAGE*?

....

Where would you *LIKE* to live?

....

Countries

```
S K R A M N E D V J A I S Z P
O A J A D A N A C M P I W F D
U I W N R M M E E Y K D E R N
T L A I D N I R E L A N D A A
H A F H J N I V U B A A E N L
A R F C E C A Y C T K L N C R
F T D D A J N L S K Y N B E E
R S Y B A W M I A C I I Z Z
I U Y P G I K O B E O F A T T
C A A B T A R V L E Z S B P I
A N H J P U D T R I L W Y W W
E L I H C T R N S A T G E Y S
L E A I N A M O R U E A I N V
N O R W A Y E A I R A G L U B
L A N E E C E E R G B M R Y M
```

AUSTRALIA	EGYPT	NEW ZEALAND
AUSTRIA	FINLAND	NORWAY
BELGIUM	FRANCE	PAKISTAN
BULGARIA	GREECE	ROMANIA
CANADA	INDIA	SOUTH AFRICA
CHILE	IRELAND	SWEDEN
CHINA	ITALY	SWITZERLAND
DENMARK	JAPAN	United States of AMERICA

About Your Home

```
E G A T T O C E E T V U Z T A
S K Y A Z Y N S N G C O R K D
W V L F G E Z T O G G A D J R
R D I E D B C Y L F D S L O D
V T M R R N G L A I T R O Y W
L L A M S B E E T E E M O H B
O G F W M B R I P D M E J B T
F U A F Y P O Y E A V S C G N
W T T R J N I V T G N U T A E
T J Z S A J I E N Y E O M R M
S O P L I L S L V O W H O A T
A B O U T D D T A I G T D G R
Y Y R M S D E C O R A T E E A
E F J P P S K A H J G L R W P
A B R S M O O R D E B E N K A
```

Tell me *ABOUT* your *HOME*.

....

Is it a *HOUSE*?

....

Is it an *APARTMENT*?

....

Is it a *COTTAGE*?

....

Is it *OLD*?

....

No, it is *NEW*.

....

Is it *MODERN*?

....

No, it is *TRADITIONAL*.

....

Is it *LARGE*?

....

Is it *SMALL*?

....

How many *BEDROOMS* does it
have?

....

Does it have a *GARAGE*?

....

Do you have some *OUTSIDE*
space?

....

Do you have a *GARDEN*?

....

Do you have any *PETS*?

....

Do you live *ALONE*?

....

No, I live with *ROOMMATES*.

....

No, I live with my *FAMILY*.

....

Do you like to *DECORATE*?

....

What is the decoration *STYLE*?

....

How long have you *LIVED* there?

....

In the House

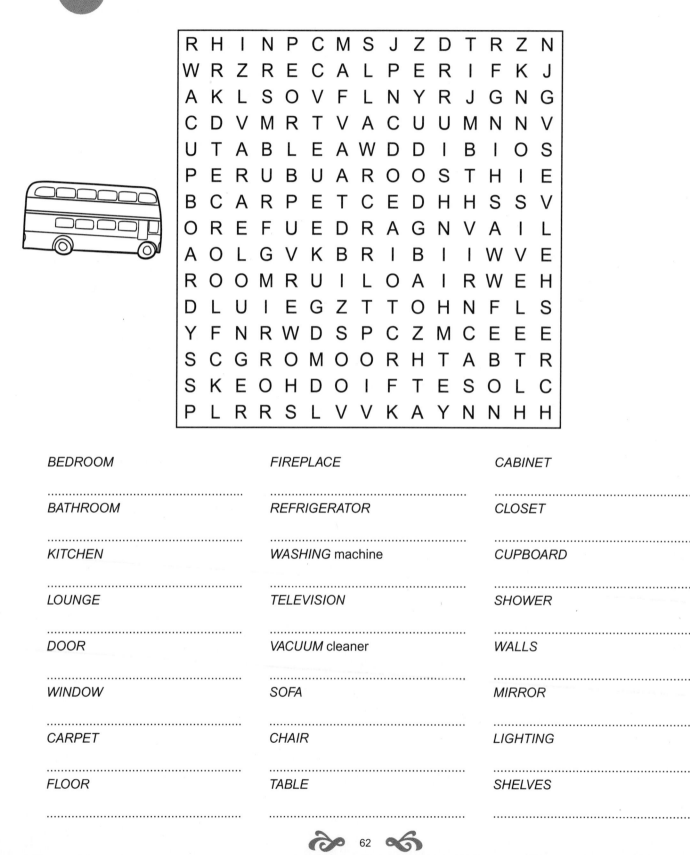

```
R H I N P C M S J Z D T R Z N
W R Z R E C A L P E R I F K J
A K L S O V F L N Y R J G N G
C D V M R T V A C U U M N N V
U T A B L E A W D D I B I O S
P E R U B U A R O O S T H I E
B C A R P E T C E D H H S S V
O R E F U E D R A G N V A I L
A O L G V K B R I B I I W V E
R O O M R U I L O A I R W E H
D L U I E G Z T T O H N F L S
Y F N R W D S P C Z M C E E E
S C G R O M O O R H T A B T R
S K E O H D O I F T E S O L C
P L R R S L V V K A Y N N H H
```

BEDROOM	FIREPLACE	CABINET
BATHROOM	REFRIGERATOR	CLOSET
KITCHEN	WASHING machine	CUPBOARD
LOUNGE	TELEVISION	SHOWER
DOOR	VACUUM cleaner	WALLS
WINDOW	SOFA	MIRROR
CARPET	CHAIR	LIGHTING
FLOOR	TABLE	SHELVES

In the Bathroom

```
W M C E G K S D K Z N E H Z P
T A I M A W L D G Y K U A Z C
O O H S A T E W P C K S I J O
O F A S G Z W S O T C S R A N
T B I D E T O T S H O I B T D
H S R H L I T R H Y M T R O I
B C D W S O R S O B B A U O T
R R R E N A P T W R Z D S T I
U U Y A O O W V E O R K H H O
S B E H N D Y H R L L I I P N
H F R G Z R O U T M I H M A E
A W E R E L B R G U T O P S R
C O O P M A H S A A O A T T O
E L I F L I A N B N O M M E B
S C I S S O R S P S T K U C J
```

TOILETRIES	BIDET	NAIL FILE
TOOTHPASTE	SHOWER	MIRROR
TOOTHBRUSH	Nail SCISSORS	COTTON wool
HAIRDRYER	RAZOR	SCRUB
TOWELS	Shaving FOAM	SPONGE
BATH	MOUTHWASH	Toilet TISSUE
SOAP	SHAMPOO	COMB
DEODORANT	CONDITIONER	HAIRBRUSH

Daily Routine

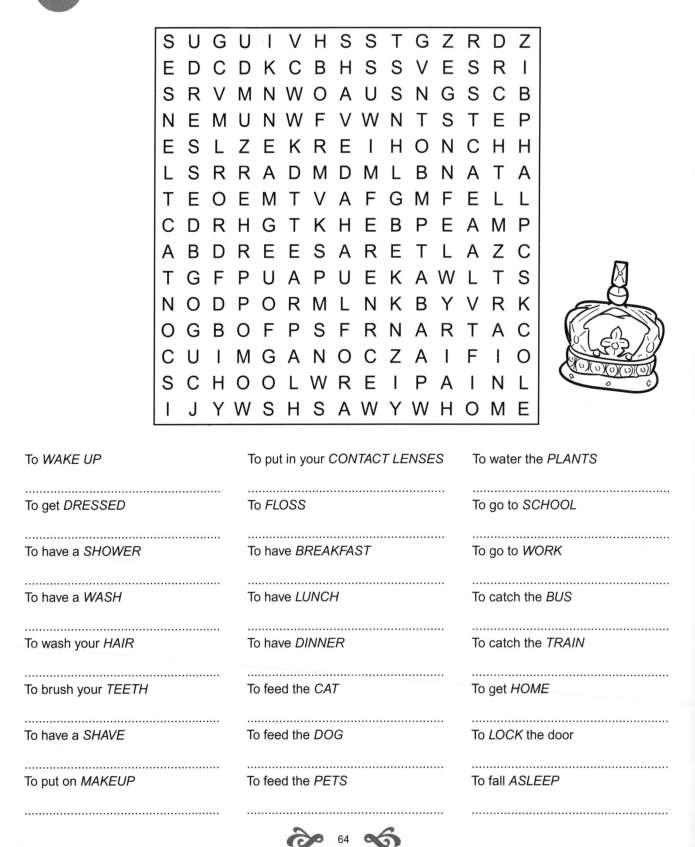

```
S U G U I V H S S T G Z R D Z
E D C D K C B H S S V E S R I
S R V M N W O A U S N G S C B
N E M U N W F V W N T S T E P
E S L Z E K R E I H O N C H H
L S R R A D M D M L B N A T A
T E O E M T V A F G M F E L L
C D R H G T K H E B P E A M P
A B D R E E S A R E T L A Z C
T G F P U A P U E K A W L T S
N O D P O R M L N K B Y V R K
O G B O F P S F R N A R T A C
C U I M G A N O C Z A I F I O
S C H O O L W R E I P A I N L
I J Y W S H S A W Y W H O M E
```

To *WAKE UP*

To get *DRESSED*

To have a *SHOWER*

To have a *WASH*

To wash your *HAIR*

To brush your *TEETH*

To have a *SHAVE*

To put on *MAKEUP*

To put in your *CONTACT LENSES*

To *FLOSS*

To have *BREAKFAST*

To have *LUNCH*

To have *DINNER*

To feed the *CAT*

To feed the *DOG*

To feed the *PETS*

To water the *PLANTS*

To go to *SCHOOL*

To go to *WORK*

To catch the *BUS*

To catch the *TRAIN*

To get *HOME*

To *LOCK* the door

To fall *ASLEEP*

Agreeing and Disagreeing

```
Y Y U R P R G Z L N E G H N T
A H C L Z M W M R I E O I I Y
S W R O N G E Y I H R M O R E
Y P A G Y T Z S Z I G E C T P
L D G A W A J S R E A K V B O
E F H J H H H B S U E I Z U S
T D O P J W H T H E O A E O S
U P O I N T E U R T L C I D I
L E Z D N D Y V H E H Z F K B
O G A W E L O G P W Y G N O L
S E V B T Z T N J A R I I B Y
B U Y C D U Z I O T H S O R F
A A A A H H A O A T U N J D V
M X B T D S B G R R E S A C V
E N J V S O S S E U G C O R A
```

Yes, you are *RIGHT*.

I could not agree with you *MORE*.

I could not agree with you *LESS*.

That is *EXACTLY* how I feel.

No *DOUBT* about it.

You have a *POINT* there.

I was *GOING* to say that.

I *GUESS* so.

Well, I am not *SURE*.

I *AGREE* with you.

I *DO NOT* agree with you.

If you *SAY* so.

You are *WRONG*.

That is not always the *CASE*.

What do you *THINK*?

OF COURSE.

MAYBE

WHAT do you think?

That is *TRUE*.

ABSOLUTELY

POSSIBLY

Society

```
E L E C T I O N U I V G C K R
R E T S I N I M E M I R P G O
Y F M A U V P N O I G I L E R
R R G P T F I N P E A C E N G
Y E T F R C T L E Y K F U D K
R A P S L I B U S Z G K M E C
M U J A U R S B N E I R P R R
E M S U P D E O O L R T E J I
D S T B D S N E N H A V I N M
I I L B P F W I T X T I A C E
C S C I E N C E A N W L C N S
I F Y E N O M T N S U A A O T
N L E T H N I C I T Y L R E S
E E M P L O Y M E N T L O C H
T N E M N R E V O G P T J V P
```

CITIZEN

CIVIL SERVANT

CLASS

CRIME

ELECTION

ENERGY

ETHNICITY

GENDER

GOVERNMENT

HEALTH service

INDUSTRY

MEDICINE

MONEY

NEWSPAPER

PEACE

PRIME MINISTER

PRISON

RELIGION

SCIENCE

EMPLOYMENT

SOCIAL group

TAXATION

VOLUNTEER

WAR

Weddings

```
T D E I R R A M M Z M U D N B
N E E Y N O I T A R B E L E C
E N N A M T S E B V M O G L L
S O N D N A B S U H C A A W G
E E O N Z Y I O E L B C E W R
R M I O E C H T K R H C D E O
P O T I E K I E T U D N I D O
D S A T T C A V R E P O R D M
E U T P V A E C I U F T B I S
G N I E Z W H P H L A N B N T
A L V C B M D P T A C V O G S
G T N E W B P R O P O S E C E
N N I R I S S E N T I W C H U
E T I E F U F K H G I F S R G
J S H R E H O N E Y M O O N W
```

To PROPOSE

To get ENGAGED

Engagement RING

HUSBAND

WIFE

MARRIED

WEDDING ring

BRIDE

GROOM

BEST MAN

Wedding DRESS

TOP HAT

To give SOMEONE away

CHURCH service

CIVIL wedding

WITNESS

RECEPTION

INVITATION

GUESTS

Wedding CAKE

PRESENT

HONEYMOON

CONFETTI

CELEBRATION

Musicians and Bands

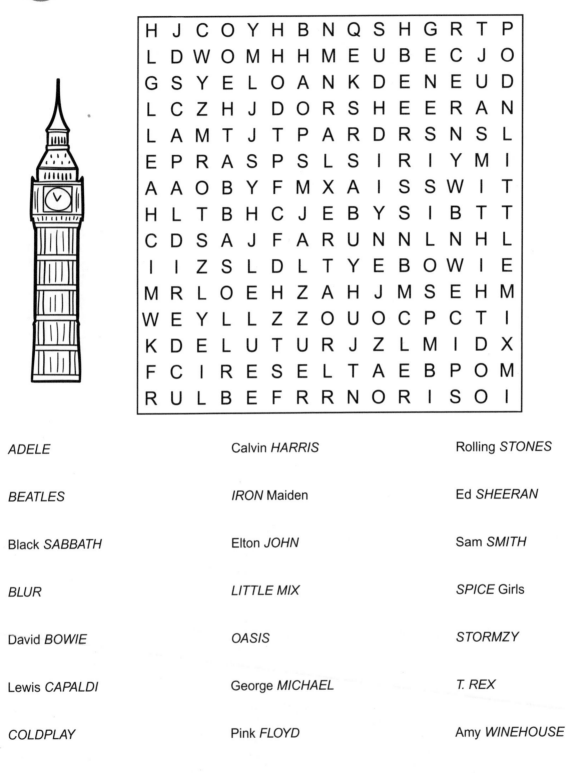

```
H J C O Y H B N Q S H G R T P
L D W O M H H M E U B E C J O
G S Y E L O A N K D E N E U D
L C Z H J D O R S H E E R A N
L A M T J T P A R D R S N S L
E P R A S P S L S I R I Y M I
A A O B Y F M X A I S S W I T
H L T B H C J E B Y S I B T T
C D S A J F A R U N N L N H L
I I Z S L D L T Y E B O W I E
M R L O E H Z A H J M S E H M
W E Y L L Z Z O U O C P C T I
K D E L U T U R J Z L M I D X
F C I R E S E L T A E B P O M
R U L B E F R R N O R I S O I
```

ADELE	Calvin *HARRIS*	Rolling *STONES*
BEATLES	*IRON* Maiden	Ed *SHEERAN*
Black *SABBATH*	Elton *JOHN*	Sam *SMITH*
BLUR	*LITTLE MIX*	*SPICE* Girls
David *BOWIE*	*OASIS*	*STORMZY*
Lewis *CAPALDI*	George *MICHAEL*	*T. REX*
COLDPLAY	Pink *FLOYD*	Amy *WINEHOUSE*
GENESIS	*QUEEN*	*ZAYN*

Pets

```
G A D H U D K F G G T N U D D
O O B C L N T F U Z O I C R Z
C A O U T T K I E R N R A V E
Z T O I U R N K D R P Z D K P
V W M W A E A R P P I E B O W
Z E B K A N I M A L U I T W G
B U J P S O H E Y W R O M S C
N H I H U M M O A D Y V K E O
R G P S C A V H W D P T L H M
A P G I N P L A L L B P A A M
B P N F C A T M Z I O D C V O
B U P F J T U S S S K N O E N
I N U F Y Z J T D G K E G Y H
T A D P W N L E G B I R G O G
C D E U M O D R R R H V A U Y
```

Do you have any *PETS*?

....

HAVE YOU ever had a pet?

....

Would you *LIKE* to get one?

....

I *WOULD* like to get one.

....

I would *NOT* like to have one.

....

I do not have *TIME* to look after a pet.

....

What *TYPE* of *ANIMAL* is it?

....

It is a *CAT*.

....

It is a *DOG*.

....

It is a *HAMSTER*.

....

It is a *LIZARD*.

....

It is a *SNAKE*.

....

It is a *RABBIT*.

....

I have a *GUINEA PIG*.

....

I would like to get a *FISH*.

....

I would like to get a *BIRD*.

....

What is its *NAME*?

....

HOW LONG have you had it?

....

Are pets *COMMON* here?

....

Hobbies and Interests

```
S M D E H Z G S W H Y V L S U
U D I I M P H Y G R J E P M S
U W A U D O V N H V V O P L L
Y F S N P E I B Y A R L B I J
P I J P C W L K R T A Y Y F W
C R I S O E I T S Y H D A E R
E N E H I M K C I P Y O B G C
G E S J M N E N A T R D V N O
N K S O U G G R H D B H N I O
H N V K E B G G G D U U L K K
S I C S R O U F U E O B S I I
E B R W T O C R A M N O B H N
V R H O H E F E L M V J G E G
D F H T S T R E C N O C O J D
O P R E G U L A R L Y B M Y W
```

What do you do in your *FREE* time?	I like to *READ*.	Have you *SEEN* …?
....	....	....
I like to *TRAVEL*.	I enjoy *COOKING*.	Is it *DUBBED*?
....	....	....
I like to *DANCE*.	I *REGULARLY* go *HIKING*.	Is it *SUBTITLED*?
....	....	....
I like to *SING*.	I enjoy *PHOTOGRAPHY*.	Did you like the film / *MOVIE*?
....	....	....
I *ENJOY* playing *SPORTS*.	I like to go *SHOPPING*.	I *THOUGHT* it was *GOOD*.
....	....	....
I like to go to *CONCERTS*.	What *MUSIC* do you like?	I did not *LIKE* it.
....	....	....
I enjoy *PLAYING* music.	What *FILMS* / movies are *SHOWING*?	
....	....	

Sports

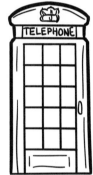

J	W	P	T	F	W	C	H	O	E	G	B	M	M	Z
B	T	N	M	D	V	M	G	Z	Z	N	S	Y	Y	U
V	A	M	Y	A	G	R	R	V	K	I	T	H	L	G
W	V	D	I	O	E	D	Z	L	Y	N	R	M	L	S
W	T	F	L	A	S	Y	L	C	T	N	O	O	A	J
Y	K	F	T	E	T	A	Y	C	I	I	P	J	B	P
G	T	K	V	Z	B	R	Y	D	L	W	S	V	T	G
A	Y	W	L	T	U	T	L	G	A	K	V	M	E	N
G	W	P	O	J	C	S	I	N	N	E	T	A	K	I
O	N	O	N	R	G	N	I	X	O	B	S	E	S	M
H	F	I	L	V	K	W	H	G	S	T	E	T	A	M
W	S	P	L	L	Y	A	L	P	R	Y	T	P	B	I
U	Y	J	K	C	O	M	O	U	E	S	T	I	W	W
H	O	F	V	F	Y	F	O	E	P	F	S	O	K	S
H	O	G	W	A	T	C	H	D	I	V	M	J	V	N

What *SPORTS* do you play?

....

I *PLAY* …

....

What sports do you *FOLLOW*?

....

I follow *BASKETBALL*.

....

FOOTBALL

....

CYCLING

....

BOXING

....

TENNIS

....

GOLF

....

I like to *WATCH* it.

....

Which sports *PERSONALITY* do you like?

....

What *TEAM* do you follow?

....

WHO is playing?

....

Who is *WINNING*?

....

Do you *WANT* to play?

....

That would be *GREAT*.

....

I have an *INJURY*.

....

Where is the nearest *SWIMMING* pool?

....

Are there tennis *COURTS* nearby?

....

Where is the local *GYM*?

....

Hiking

```
Z T E S N J E B E A K H F V U
A F G Y C H T T H N Y R V V C
T B A S W D T S U J Y E H H G
K F L W M A A A O O E Z B W C
K Z L I F A I Y P L R D M E H
G N I T S E R E T N I F K G C
H A V L Z G I K J U O I U W E
B Y B K B N O C E W H O G D T
C T L U C I F F I D R E I I D
D T S E T R O H S H A U D D P
C B I C B B V C T S G A L C R
T R A I L S W V I S C E N I C
C A M P S I T E N N E D R P M
U S N Z I F S D Y J T W U A G
J O B C N T D S E I L P P U S
```

Are there hiking *TRAILS*?

....

Do we need a *GUIDE*?

....

Where can I buy *SUPPLIES*?

....

Do you have a *MAP*?

....

How long is the *HIKE*?

....

Is it *DIFFICULT*?

....

Is it well *MARKED*?

....

What do I need to *BRING*?

....

Is it *SCENIC*?

....

Which *ROUTE* is *EASIEST*?

....

Which route is *SHORTEST*?

....

Which route is most *INTERESTING*?

....

Where is the *CAMPSITE*?

....

Where is the *VILLAGE*?

....

Does this *PATH* go to …?

....

Can we go *THROUGH* here?

....

I am *LOST*.

....

Music

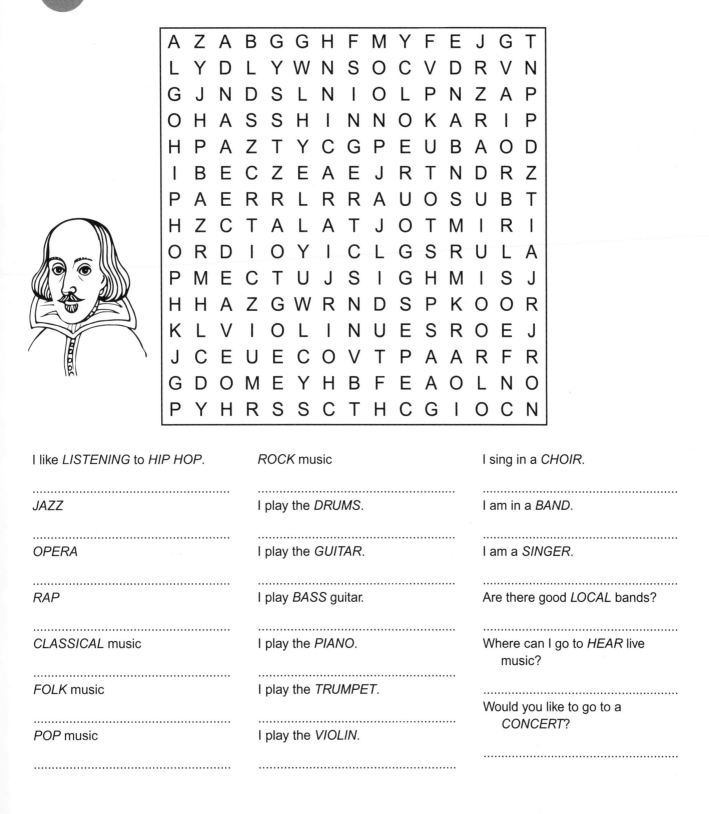

```
A Z A B G G H F M Y F E J G T
L Y D L Y W N S O C V D R V N
G J N D S L N I O L P N Z A P
O H A S S H I N N O K A R I P
H P A Z T Y C G P E U B A O D
I B E C Z E A E J R T N D R Z
P A E R R L R R A U O S U B T
H Z C T A L A T J O T M I R I
O R D I O Y I C L G S R U L A
P M E C T U J S I G H M I S J
H H A Z G W R N D S P K O O R
K L V I O L I N U E S R O E J
J C E U E C O V T P A A R F R
G D O M E Y H B F E A O L N O
P Y H R S S C T H C G I O C N
```

I like *LISTENING* to *HIP HOP*.

....

JAZZ

....

OPERA

....

RAP

....

CLASSICAL music

....

FOLK music

....

POP music

....

ROCK music

....

I play the *DRUMS*.

....

I play the *GUITAR*.

....

I play *BASS* guitar.

....

I play the *PIANO*.

....

I play the *TRUMPET*.

....

I play the *VIOLIN*.

....

I sing in a *CHOIR*.

....

I am in a *BAND*.

....

I am a *SINGER*.

....

Are there good *LOCAL* bands?

....

Where can I go to *HEAR* live
music?

....

Would you like to go to a
CONCERT?

....

Artists

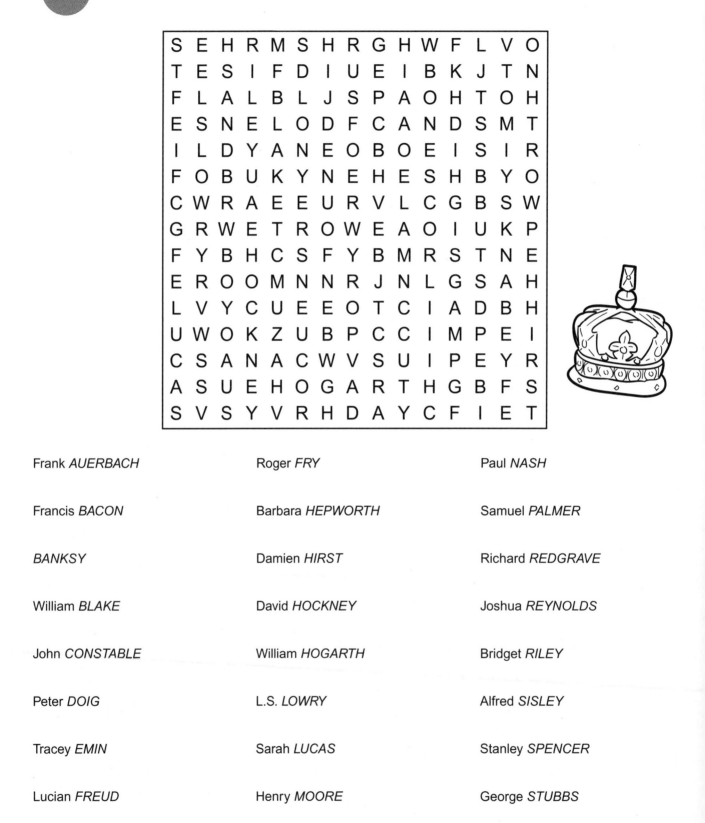

S	E	H	R	M	S	H	R	G	H	W	F	L	V	O
T	E	S	I	F	D	I	U	E	I	B	K	J	T	N
F	L	A	L	B	L	J	S	P	A	O	H	T	O	H
E	S	N	E	L	O	D	F	C	A	N	D	S	M	T
I	L	D	Y	A	N	E	O	B	O	E	I	S	I	R
F	O	B	U	K	Y	N	E	H	E	S	H	B	Y	O
C	W	R	A	E	E	U	R	V	L	C	G	B	S	W
G	R	W	E	T	R	O	W	E	A	O	I	U	K	P
F	Y	B	H	C	S	F	Y	B	M	R	S	T	N	E
E	R	O	O	M	N	N	R	J	N	L	G	S	A	H
L	V	Y	C	U	E	E	O	T	C	I	A	D	B	H
U	W	O	K	Z	U	B	P	C	C	I	M	P	E	I
C	S	A	N	A	C	W	V	S	U	I	P	E	Y	R
A	S	U	E	H	O	G	A	R	T	H	G	B	F	S
S	V	S	Y	V	R	H	D	A	Y	C	F	I	E	T

Frank AUERBACH

Francis BACON

BANKSY

William BLAKE

John CONSTABLE

Peter DOIG

Tracey EMIN

Lucian FREUD

Roger FRY

Barbara HEPWORTH

Damien HIRST

David HOCKNEY

William HOGARTH

L.S. LOWRY

Sarah LUCAS

Henry MOORE

Paul NASH

Samuel PALMER

Richard REDGRAVE

Joshua REYNOLDS

Bridget RILEY

Alfred SISLEY

Stanley SPENCER

George STUBBS

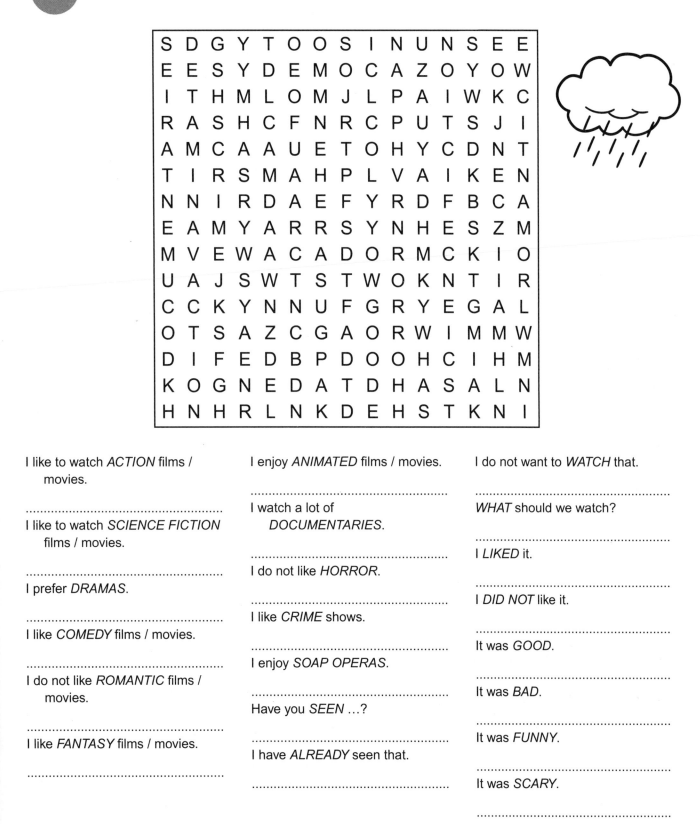

I like to watch *ACTION* films / movies.

....

I like to watch *SCIENCE FICTION* films / movies.

....

I prefer *DRAMAS*.

....

I like *COMEDY* films / movies.

....

I do not like *ROMANTIC* films / movies.

....

I like *FANTASY* films / movies.

....

I enjoy *ANIMATED* films / movies.

....

I watch a lot of *DOCUMENTARIES*.

....

I do not like *HORROR*.

....

I like *CRIME* shows.

....

I enjoy *SOAP OPERAS*.

....

Have you *SEEN* ...?

....

I have *ALREADY* seen that.

....

I do not want to *WATCH* that.

....

WHAT should we watch?

....

I *LIKED* it.

....

I *DID NOT* like it.

....

It was *GOOD*.

....

It was *BAD*.

....

It was *FUNNY*.

....

It was *SCARY*.

....

Popular Culture

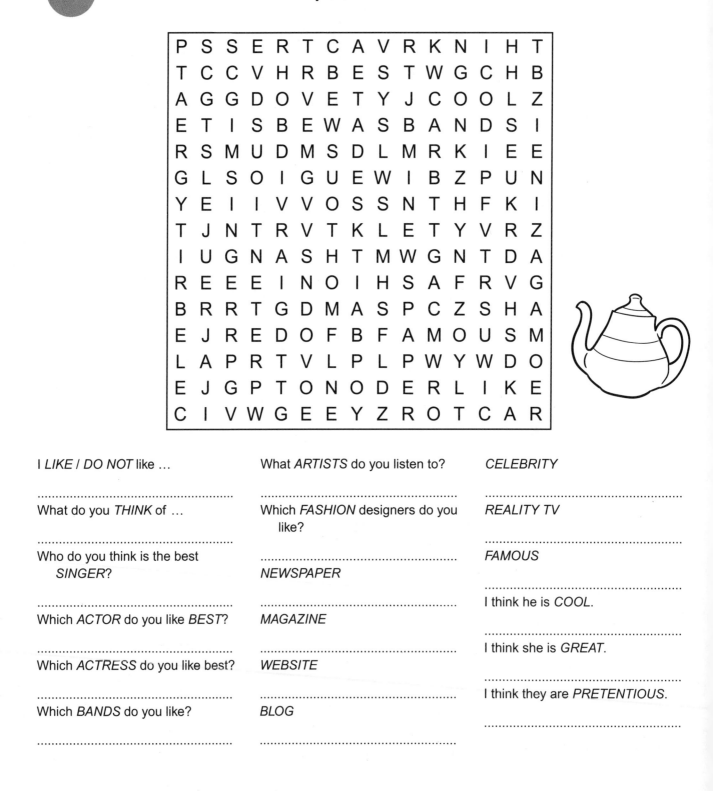

```
P S S E R T C A V R K N I H T
T C C V H R B E S T W G C H B
A G G D O V E T Y J C O O L Z
E T I S B E W A S B A N D S I
R S M U D M S D L M R K I E E
G L S O I G U E W I B Z P U N
Y E I I V V O S S N T H F K I
T J N T R V T K L E T Y V R Z
I U G N A S H T M W G N T D A
R E E E I N O I H S A F R V G
B R R T G D M A S P C Z S H A
E J R E D O F B F A M O U S M
L A P R T V L P L P W Y W D O
E J G P T O N O D E R L I K E
C I V W G E E Y Z R O T C A R
```

I *LIKE / DO NOT* like …

....

What do you *THINK* of …

....

Who do you think is the best *SINGER*?

....

Which *ACTOR* do you like *BEST*?

....

Which *ACTRESS* do you like best?

....

Which *BANDS* do you like?

....

What *ARTISTS* do you listen to?

....

Which *FASHION* designers do you like?

....

NEWSPAPER

....

MAGAZINE

....

WEBSITE

....

BLOG

....

CELEBRITY

....

REALITY TV

....

FAMOUS

....

I think he is *COOL*.

....

I think she is *GREAT*.

....

I think they are *PRETENTIOUS*.

....

At the Pool

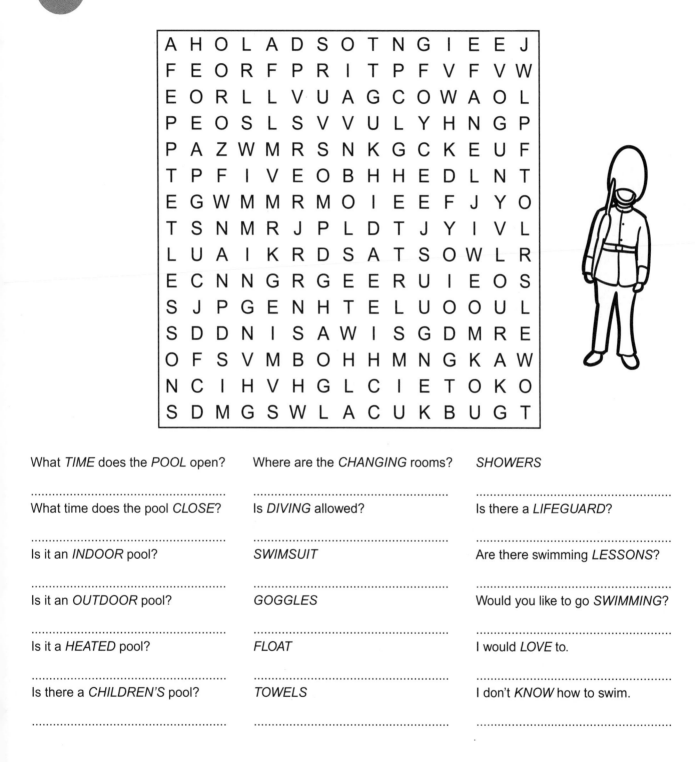

A	H	O	L	A	D	S	O	T	N	G	I	E	E	J
F	E	O	R	F	P	R	I	T	P	F	V	F	V	W
E	O	R	L	L	V	U	A	G	C	O	W	A	O	L
P	E	O	S	L	S	V	V	U	L	Y	H	N	G	P
P	A	Z	W	M	R	S	N	K	G	C	K	E	U	F
T	P	F	I	V	E	O	B	H	H	E	D	L	N	T
E	G	W	M	M	R	M	O	I	E	E	F	J	Y	O
T	S	N	M	R	J	P	L	D	T	J	Y	I	V	L
L	U	A	I	K	R	D	S	A	T	S	O	W	L	R
E	C	N	N	G	R	E	E	R	U	I	E	O	S
S	J	P	G	E	N	H	T	E	L	U	O	O	U	L
S	D	D	N	I	S	A	W	I	S	G	D	M	R	E
O	F	S	V	M	B	O	H	H	M	N	G	K	A	W
N	C	I	H	V	H	G	L	C	I	E	T	O	K	O
S	D	M	G	S	W	L	A	C	U	K	B	U	G	T

What *TIME* does the *POOL* open?

....

What time does the pool *CLOSE*?

....

Is it an *INDOOR* pool?

....

Is it an *OUTDOOR* pool?

....

Is it a *HEATED* pool?

....

Is there a *CHILDREN'S* pool?

....

Where are the *CHANGING* rooms?

....

Is *DIVING* allowed?

....

SWIMSUIT

....

GOGGLES

....

FLOAT

....

TOWELS

....

SHOWERS

....

Is there a *LIFEGUARD*?

....

Are there swimming *LESSONS*?

....

Would you like to go *SWIMMING*?

....

I would *LOVE* to.

....

I don't *KNOW* how to swim.

....

The Royal Family

```
E I Z Y P H I L L I P S B B C
R F H I W I L L I A M E D U H
A U Y O D C A F Z P G L W C A
H I O N L D O B I C E I I K R
N D I L N Y A R A S N Z N I L
E N Y I O L R M O D C A V N O
G E T E M C I O S N L B E G T
E B L O U L I O O R A E S H T
S E R I L G R U C D R T T A E
E A D A B G E O R G E H I M A
L T R L R U A N P K N I T O V
R R A O I I J R I F C I U F N
A I W U E R I G D E E C R O K
H C D I A N M E R E E R E D O
C E E S P A A N N E N K T V D
```

ANMER Hall	*CLARENCE* House	*INVESTITURE*
Princess *ANNE*	*CORONATION*	*JUBILEE*
BALMORAL Castle	Queen *ELIZABETH II*	Prince *LOUIS*
Princess *BEATRICE*	Prince *EDWARD*	Peter *PHILLIPS*
BUCKINGHAM Palace	Princess *EUGENIE*	Zara *TINDALL*
CAMILLA, Duchess of Cornwall	*GARDEN* parties	Trooping the *COLOUR*
Prince *CHARLES*	Prince *GEORGE*	Prince *WILLIAM*
Princess *CHARLOTTE*	*HOLYROOD* Palace	*WINDSOR* Castle

Going Out

```
D J Z R A F E R D R A W R O F
A V O A Y M Y R A O K U H W V
N N A B C A T G T J I L E U S
C W N E W O E E S D L E E B A
I E H P N L E E J L K A U T Z
N A A I S M I F E I L Z I S
G A G Y B R A E N A C I D M I
F H E H H V D D E A C S U E E
T E J P T N A R U A T S E R R
H R L Z O I G A Y Z L Y R Y E
N I G H T C L U B P T L R E H
K R R C R A L L S A L R I T W
P C C O T A M O E B O A M W R
F J I E Z E N R C S M I C G I
E I R P B E G P T K K L T E R
```

What is on *NEARBY*?	*WHERE* should we meet?	Where can we go *DANCING*?
What is on *TONIGHT*?	*LET'S* meet at the …	This *PLACE* is *GREAT*.
What is on this *WEEKEND*?	Where *WILL* you be?	Let's go to a *NIGHTCLUB*.
Where are the *CLUBS*?	I will *PICK* you up.	Let's go to a *BAR*.
What *TIME* would you like to meet?	See you *LATER*.	Let's go to a *CAFE*.
I would like to *MEET* at … O'CLOCK.	I am looking *FORWARD* to it.	Let's go to a *RESTAURANT*.
	SORRY I'm late.	

Feelings and Opinions

```
G B F D E S U F N O C L B L G
B U N Z M E L B O R P O N N M
Y P P A H O D E L P O E P Z V
A V E R A G E Y F C N S I D E
H W O C E M K E K T O M H X P
F E Y F W A I S E C M H C O P
U J R N U N L R L I L E E G W
N D I D N O T E G W L U M D R
N A Y C F A V R C L I M A T E
Y F C Z I E A B E C O N O M Y
U M E N R T B N S S O C U A D
F V I E I N T H O U G H T A C
I N K O L A V E E R G A S I D
G S N Z U R M Y L E A B M E U
O F C O U R S E S R U P F E I
```

Did you like the *SHOW*?	I *LIKED* it.	I am *SAD*.
....	....	....
I *THOUGHT* it was *ENTERTAINING*.	I *DID NOT* like it.	I am *CONFUSED*.
....	....	....
I thought it was *FUNNY*.	I *DISAGREE*.	I am not *SURE*.
....	....	....
I thought it was *EXCELLENT*.	*YES*, but …	How do *PEOPLE* feel about the *ECONOMY*?
....	....	....
I thought it was *CLEVER*.	*OF COURSE*.	How do people *FEEL* about *IMMIGRATION*?
....	....	....
I thought it was *AVERAGE*.	*NO PROBLEM*.	How do people feel about *CLIMATE* change?
....	....	....
	I am *HAPPY*.	
	....	

Beliefs and Culture

```
E K Y A R P B U D D H I S T B
N G V T K W Z V W B T S P E C
H S E C N G K P Y M R V I A O
I G N I T S E R E T N I T K M
N A G N O S T I C U Z H T I H
D L H C C I A T T U O B A S N
U D Y Z A T J R E L I G I O N
C T U S H G T E I C U S T O M
T B S E F J Y C W H W J B L E
A F I N R E L I G I O U S L F
L S Y O I L I M I L S U M E R
T T K I O A M L M C E H L T T
W L W D I R G D E D N E F F O
U Y R R O S R A J B K G L T P
I Z R P F D N A I T S I R H C
```

What is your *RELIGION*?	I am *JEWISH*.	Can I *PRAY* here?
I am *AGNOSTIC*.	I am *HINDU*.	Is this a local *CUSTOM*?
I am an *ATHEIST*.	I am a *BUDDHIST*.	It is very *INTERESTING*.
I am *CATHOLIC*.	I am a *SIKH*.	I would like to *TRY* it.
I am a *CHRISTIAN*.	I am not *RELIGIOUS*.	I am *SORRY* if I *OFFENDED* you.
I am a *MUSLIM*.	It is *AGAINST* my *BELIEFS*.	Could you *TELL* me more *ABOUT* it?

Shakespeare

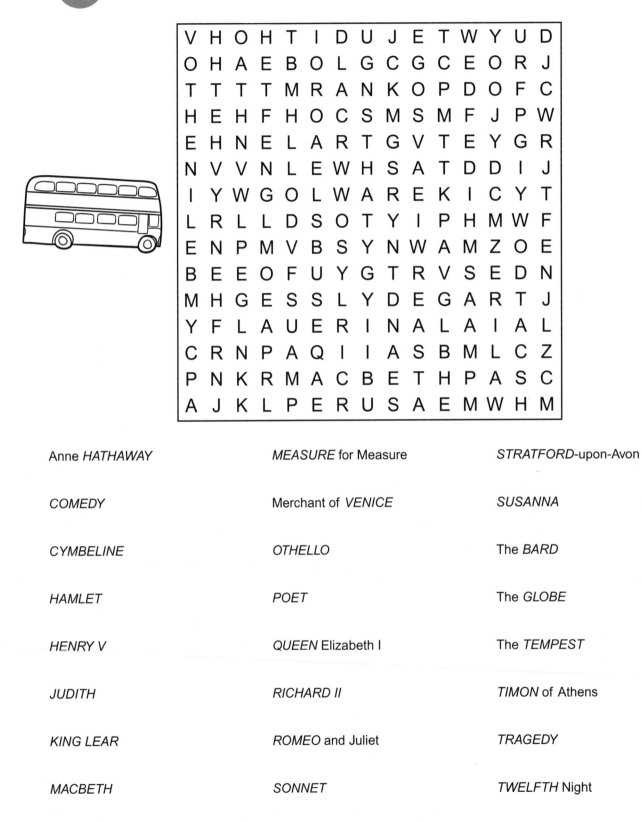

```
V H O H T I D U J E T W Y U D
O H A E B O L G C G C E O R J
T T T T M R A N K O P D O F C
H E H F H O C S M S M F J P W
E H N E L A R T G V T E Y G R
N V V N L E W H S A T D D I J
I Y W G O L W A R E K I C Y T
L R L L D S O T Y I P H M W F
E N P M V B S Y N W A M Z O E
B E E O F U Y G T R V S E D N
M H G E S S L Y D E G A R T J
Y F L A U E R I N A L A I A L
C R N P A Q I I A S B M L C Z
P N K R M A C B E T H P A S C
A J K L P E R U S A E M W H M
```

Anne *HATHAWAY*	*MEASURE* for Measure	*STRATFORD*-upon-Avon
COMEDY	Merchant of *VENICE*	*SUSANNA*
CYMBELINE	*OTHELLO*	The *BARD*
HAMLET	*POET*	The *GLOBE*
HENRY V	*QUEEN* Elizabeth I	The *TEMPEST*
JUDITH	*RICHARD II*	*TIMON* of Athens
KING LEAR	*ROMEO* and Juliet	*TRAGEDY*
MACBETH	*SONNET*	*TWELFTH* Night

Nature

```
L F I C F A T D D W M C R A S
Z E I S H N T S E Y R K O S V
Y M A R J A G N E I L C V A B
E K R F E V W R V R E T L H R
E D S B M H A E A A O L T U Y
R E F P W D R F N S E F J T P
T K H J N L P A A Y S P N E L
S A I A Y E K D A V L V I N A
G L L H C A E B U V S C A A G
E S L N L T R Z O N J A R L I
I K Y N N U L Z O B K W N P W
A P G A W L K W V U S S G D I
N N L E Y T N I A T N U O M N
N P J M A H T R A E U L U I D
P F L O W E R C E V A W V J L
```

BEACH	LAKE	SAND
EARTH	LEAF	SKY
FIRE	MOUNTAIN	SNOW
FLOWER	OCEAN	SOIL
FOREST	PLANET	TREE
GRASS	PLANT	VALLEY
HILL	RAIN	WAVE
ISLAND	RIVER	WIND

Creatures

```
T B F P K U E D H G J S Y U F
E U Z B C D C H O O F K A Z F
T T G G U A A S R A R W P C U
O T I C Y O Y O P T D S B H Z
R E K R S M T J T I D E E O S
T R R G A A O A N H D Y O U W
O F L D G G S F A M A E P S T
I L D I V P E R W R I O R E R
S Y L M I A A O S E T F D F T
E L W G W M L G U C K P R L J
A T R A B B I T O A S A T Y W
T D G B U L L S L C A G N F H
U P E C I F C A D I U Q S S A
D M O E C O E L E P H A N T L
B W W B R X H N I H P L O D E
```

ALLIGATOR	FOX	SEAL
BULL	FROG	SNAKE
BUTTERFLY	GOAT	SPIDER
COW	HORSE	SQUID
DEER	HOUSEFLY	SWAN
DOLPHIN	OCTOPUS	TOAD
DUCK	PIG	TORTOISE
ELEPHANT	RABBIT	WHALE

Plants and Trees

```
N R H J F R Y F P S G D A Z N
J E C W S E E B U S H S C Y Y
O T L V R U E H G R S I S B B
C M Y L M O N R T Z Z I O R M
A W R P O J W F T A A F E A K
L I L Y P P W K L D E D U L K
Z P F E A O R O A O N H I W Z
W G T M N A P F Y E W B N G M
P A B L D R F M V Y E E S V E
L T I E R O O A L E P Z R N K
B O C R D A L H C N I L F A H
O O Y I M S I H T C L Y A B Z
P R L E A F L V A T U B H N T
V G I F H C A R N A T I O N T
V I O L E T C H E S T N U T J
```

TREE	OAK	CARNATION
BUSH	ELM	LILY
PLANT	CEDAR	SUNFLOWER
LEAF	BEECH	DAFFODIL
THORN	CHESTNUT	POPPY
ROOT	TULIP	LILAC
PETAL	DAISY	HEATHER
POLLEN	VIOLET	LAVENDER

Geographical Features

```
F E V C T S E R O F G P I O Y
D L A N D Z P D J U P M C N V
E V U E P B D E C S T A L R A
E V L G E L G E N F Y W I I L
R T V A D N A L S I R S F V L
A I C U N E A T P E N I F E E
L H A J I I R E E Z R S T R Y
L N M F S E D C Z A V T U A W
A I L H A T N A D I U L P L V
F A S M B O U N H I C I L Y A
R T C O A S T Y I F J V E N F
E N Y J Z D J O L R G L I V M
T U K K C T L N L D H A Y S G
A O I O N A C L O V L L Z A E
W M N Y O G A L E P I H C R A
```

ARCHIPELAGO	DESERT	PLATEAU
BASIN	FOREST	RIVER
BEACH	GULF	STREAM
CANYON	HILL	SWAMP
CAVE	ISLAND	TUNDRA
CLIFF	MOUNTAIN	VALLEY
COAST	PENINSULA	VOLCANO
DELTA	PLAIN	WATERFALL

Cities

```
W N R M D Z S K T D U N D E E
C O B A B E R D E E N J O F V
S D R H N O E S T A L E E D S
W N I G Y L H G R U B N I D E
A O S N P I C L D R O F X O V
N L T I S N S A O I P H A Y R
S L O M N C D P R B R Z A N E
E E L R J O P L H D C B S G T
A I F I J L T A E O I A M W S
R C A B K N C H V I L F O A A
B E L F A S T E G F F G F B C
H S V Y N H N H O I S F P A N
R T E X E T E R E A R M E T A
H E H P R J D O L G U B N H L
R R Z Y B A N G O R C A S F S
```

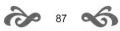

ABERDEEN	CARDIFF	LEICESTER
BANGOR	COVENTRY	LINCOLN
BATH	DUNDEE	LONDON
BELFAST	EDINBURGH	OXFORD
BIRMINGHAM	EXETER	SALFORD
BRIGHTON	GLASGOW	SHEFFIELD
BRISTOL	LEEDS	SWANSEA
CAMBRIDGE	LANCASTER	YORK

Emergencies

```
D E F S M K L R L G R O C R N
G C T H Y G Y S S A B M E Y E
Y I B S T L N E Z P T Q H M M
P L E H M G R K A U U Z E L H
D O L Z L V B S A I R R A O F
N P N P I E S J R D G G S Z I
M D J C A P C E E E C P E H R
R D E D O E D N N R I E F N S
T O D R N T E C A T K I G F T
G K T V U P Y S A L R O H E A
O E S C P J H L R E U Z U I I
A M L A O E N J T T P B S H D
W B H O D D H I F G M Y M T S
A R G S C C Y D G O H N P A Y
Y Z S T A T I O N C G K K P T
```

HELP!

....

Please *GO AWAY*.

....

LET GO!

....

Stop, *THIEF*!

....

It is an *EMERGENCY*.

....

Do you have a *FIRST AID* kit?

....

Call the *POLICE*.

....

Call a *DOCTOR*.

....

Call an *AMBULANCE*.

....

Call the fire *SERVICE*.

....

What service do you *REQUIRE*?

....

What *HAPPENED*?

....

Someone is *INJURED*.

....

There is a *FIRE*.

....

It is very *URGENT*.

....

Where is the *EMBASSY*?

....

Where is the *HOSPITAL*?

....

Where is the police *STATION*?

....

I have lost my *PASSPORT*.

....

I have *CRASHED* my car.

....

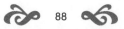

Police

83

```
N E L I M Z T O N N A C V H S
O N K R G Z L T M J Y C O F S
I O A K E O P I C F U I C U L
T E R U R H H O Y C A R I S O
A M A W D E G G U M J T R T O
C O D P A S J J E A C T S O K
I S H V O L B Z I A L R Z L L
F Y N H Y L L P S S C O V E I
I L K A U P I E F W W P H N K
T D E P R T U C T I E S S D E
N M N P N B W R E T M S I E I
E G O E N V C W S N T A L B T
D A H N F Y L H F E U P G B A
I B P L E T U P J S D O N O I
J L R N D Y O N E S M K E R Y
```

Where is the *POLICE* station?

....

I have been *ROBBED*.

....

I have been *MUGGED*.

....

What did he / she *LOOK LIKE*?

....

Was there a *WITNESS*?

....

Where did it *HAPPEN*?

....

It was *HIM*.

....

It was *HER*.

....

SOMEONE has stolen my *BAG*.

....

Someone has stolen my *PURSE*.

....

Someone has stolen my *MONEY*.

....

Someone has stolen my *SUITCASE*.

....

Someone has stolen my *PHONE*.

....

Someone has stolen my *WALLET*.

....

Someone has *STOLEN* my passport.

....

Someone has stolen my *CAR*.

....

Where is your *IDENTIFICATION*?

....

Here is my *PASSPORT*.

....

I *CANNOT* speak *ENGLISH*.

....

89

Health

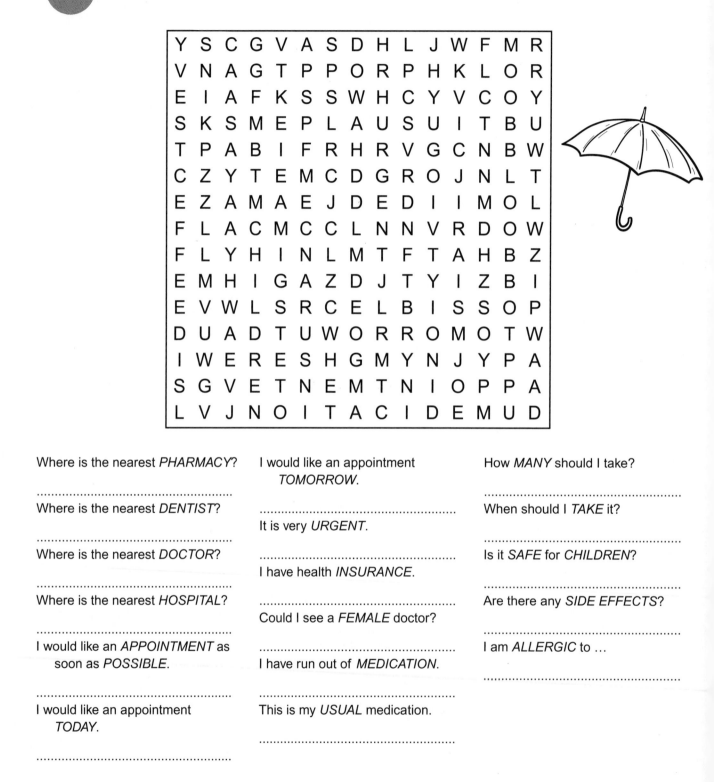

```
Y S C G V A S D H L J W F M R
V N A G T P P O R P H K L O R
E I A F K S S W H C Y V C O Y
S K S M E P L A U S U I T B U
T P A B I F R H R V G C N B W
C Z Y T E M C D G R O J N L T
E Z A M A E J D E D I I M O L
F L A C M C C L N N V R D O W
F L Y H I N L M T F T A H B Z
E M H I G A Z D J T Y I Z B I
E V W L S R C E L B I S S O P
D U A D T U W O R R O M O T W
I W E R E S H G M Y N J Y P A
S G V E T N E M T N I O P P A
L V J N O I T A C I D E M U D
```

Where is the nearest *PHARMACY*?

....

Where is the nearest *DENTIST*?

....

Where is the nearest *DOCTOR*?

....

Where is the nearest *HOSPITAL*?

....

I would like an *APPOINTMENT* as soon as *POSSIBLE*.

....

I would like an appointment *TODAY*.

....

I would like an appointment *TOMORROW*.

....

It is very *URGENT*.

....

I have health *INSURANCE*.

....

Could I see a *FEMALE* doctor?

....

I have run out of *MEDICATION*.

....

This is my *USUAL* medication.

....

How *MANY* should I take?

....

When should I *TAKE* it?

....

Is it *SAFE* for *CHILDREN*?

....

Are there any *SIDE EFFECTS*?

....

I am *ALLERGIC* to …

....

Illnesses and Symptoms

```
U O G N Z R Y L W E B W Z H I
J F J Y A H R M B H E S V G B
M E K S L G E T O H K N K N V
F L H J W U V A C S A O O I H
I L Y R M O I A A S E I W T L
S T U N G C H B I E W T H I U
H C A M O T S C S H P A E M A
R I S I O F K R I I E P A O L
T J N O A E O H R R A I D V L
A U T J B W S B M B R T A P E
O S T R U H B I L Z A S C D R
R F E V E R H G C W C N H I G
H N O I T C E F N I H O E Z Y
T M R G N C P D L O E C K Z K
Y A M H T S A L K V G U J Y I
```

I am *SICK*.

I have recently had *FLU*.

It *HURTS* here.

I have been *INJURED*.

I *FELL*.

I have been *VOMITING*.

I have a *RASH*.

I have an *ALLERGY*.

I have *FEVER*.

I have *ASTHMA*.

I have *DIARRHOEA*.

I have a *HEADACHE*.

I have an *INFECTION*.

I have a *STOMACH* ache.

I have *EARACHE*.

I have a sore *THROAT*.

I have a *COUGH*.

I have *CONSTIPATION*.

I have a *TOOTHACHE*.

I have been *STUNG*.

I feel *SHIVERY*.

I feel *WEAK*.

I feel *DIZZY*.

I feel *WORSE*.

Body Parts

```
A V J N B B J C N S L E E H I
M S I W E O P A Y G C R M R B
B H Z R C U K O W B B A M O Y
C R S I W H R H C A M O T S P
U P Y S I O J N C L O U C V W
R G N T R P B K Z E U L H R Y
N T O T B P J L G J T D E T Y
S I A U D G L G E S H G S G C
A K V O N D A E H E N H T H H
G S I A R J K O E I F A C E E
K C E N W H U N F G S H P S E
F V T K P L T Z E E T O M S K
G H J L D A R M F E S U T M J
Y R U E D N A H G B Y O J K U
M W R N G F N G Y H F I N J M
```

ANKLE	FINGER	NECK
ARM	HAND	NOSE
BACK	HEAD	SHOULDER
CHEEK	HEEL	SKIN
CHEST	JAW	STOMACH
CHIN	KNEE	THROAT
ELBOW	LEG	THUMB
FACE	MOUTH	WRIST

Problems

```
C I H T E L L A W W A T L E R
P O B R O K E N D O W N Z G E
D R N B L O G R U K B H A A T
E E K F E Y L E N D L L U G U
I P T C U U F I D C T L Z G P
R A N D Z S M J A E D M I U M
R I T E G R E M J E R O A L O
O R R L Y V E D Y T E U H B C
W E O L A R D A Y Z A S J W T
W D P E A F L I G H T F R N H
P W S C W E R E E N O H P U I
M M S N D P H T T N Z R R J P
W L A A V V E M O O R T S O L
H S P C K T L F D N H P J A R
O U O I B H P P P I D F M L R
```

I am *LOST*.

....

I am *HURT*.

....

I am *INJURED*.

....

I am *ILL*.

....

I am *CONFUSED*.

....

I am *WORRIED*.

....

Can you *HELP* me?

....

Can I use your *PHONE*?

....

I have lost my *LUGGAGE*.

....

I have lost my *PASSPORT*.

....

I have lost my *WALLET*.

....

I have lost my *PURSE*.

....

My *CAMERA* needs to be repaired.

....

My *COMPUTER* needs to be
repaired.

....

My smartphone needs to be
REPAIRED.

....

My car has *BROKEN DOWN*.

....

I have missed my *FLIGHT*.

....

I do not like my *HOTEL*.

....

I do not like my *ROOM*.

....

I have *JETLAG*.

....

My flight is *DELAYED*.

....

My flight has been *CANCELLED*.

....

Eating Out

```
L J I Y D K F K B B D R Z M R
L G N I V R E S H O F L R N E
D L F H Y Z B R O W W U E D C
T G B R E A K F A S T F Y I O
N U P J K S O E F T A R S N M
A R U M E N U R S C P G E N M
R R H O O O A I E E L T L E E
U R Y F C U L G O S R N B R N
A J J F N J B P L K E G A N D
T A B A W N L U B P C R T B Z
S V D E T E N A T D F O V H F
E S C E K C R U I R H O L E R
R U H R H I C D A I U F V C C
K M D E S O L C W N K V P E O
C K U P N A K S O K V I E R F
```

BREAKFAST

....

LUNCH

....

DINNER

....

FOOD

....

DRINK

....

I would LIKE …

....

Can you RECOMMEND a BAR?

....

Can you recommend a CAFE?

....

Can you recommend a RESTAURANT?

....

Are you still SERVING food?

....

Sorry, we are CLOSED.

....

We have no free TABLES.

....

I would like to RESERVE a table.

....

For … PEOPLE.

....

At … O'CLOCK.

....

How long is the WAIT?

....

I would like the drinks LIST, please.

....

I would like the MENU, please.

....

94

On the Menu

```
M Y U W D W J Y K S M F T D S
A S P A R L B N P N O G J C T
I K P R H O B K T N A U Z L E
N N A I I V S R A P P S P V A
C I Y L C A Y G P M E D I U M
O R E M L Y E E G V U D D G E
U D O A V V T D E O E E R J D
R T D A T I E G N I S I E W E
S F T W S F E T R S L R T E T
E O D E F T H F E L E R T L A
S S R U A E E R E T A F A L N
U S T R S N T D R R T M B D I
R S I I V A Y A E G I J N O R
H A D E W E T J T L C S I N A
N E I E M S E Y D T H A F E M
```

APPETISERS	MEDIUM	SOUP
BOILED	MILD	SPICY
DESSERT	ON THE SIDE	STARTER
FRIED	RARE	STEAMED
GRILLED	RAW	STUFFED
IN BATTER	ROASTED	VEGAN
MAIN COURSES	SALAD	VEGETARIAN
MARINATED	SOFT DRINKS	WELL DONE

Drinks

```
E O D Z D E L Z P P A S U Z O
Z Y S R Y E J Z I I H C M P T
L T I S A R L Z C U T V U V A
E A B W E W O L R H D C R Y M
M Y C L I R N T U D E U E D O
O G H D A O P R P M C K R N T
N N O C P C N S B A I F K A E
A I C M P I K I E O G L E R T
D L O R R S N R C R T E K B I
E K L P E S T E E C F T D F H
S R A O G A G E A F U E L D W
T A T M N L N B O P R P D E V
I P E C A G P C Y K P P P Z W
L S J C R E N V J S N L Z A V
L C I N O T D N A N I G E E C
```

BEER	GLASS	PINEAPPLE juice
BLACK coffee	GREEN tea	RED wine
BOTTLE	Hot CHOCOLATE	RUM
BRANDY	ICED coffee	SPARKLING water
CAPPUCCINO	LEMONADE	STILL water
CUP	MILK	TOMATO juice
ESPRESSO	MULLED wine	White COFFEE
GIN AND TONIC	ORANGE juice	WHITE wine

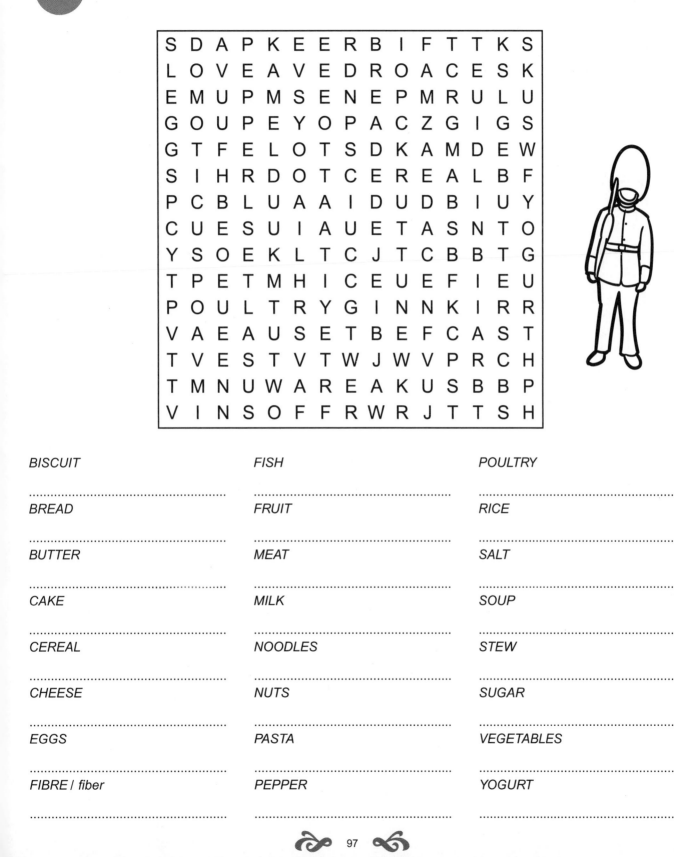

Food

```
S D A P K E E R B I F T T K S
L O V E A V E D R O A C E S K
E M U P M S E N E P M R U L U
G O U P E Y O P A C Z G I G S
G T F E L O T S D K A M D E W
S I H R D O T C E R E A L B F
P C B L U A A I D U D B I U Y
C U E S U I A U E T A S N T O
Y S O E K L T C J T C B B T G
T P E T M H I C E U E F I E U
P O U L T R Y G I N N K I R R
V A E A U S E T B E F C A S T
T V E S T V T W J W V P R C H
T M N U W A R E A K U S B B P
V I N S O F F R W R J T T S H
```

BISCUIT	FISH	POULTRY
BREAD	FRUIT	RICE
BUTTER	MEAT	SALT
CAKE	MILK	SOUP
CEREAL	NOODLES	STEW
CHEESE	NUTS	SUGAR
EGGS	PASTA	VEGETABLES
FIBRE / fiber	PEPPER	YOGURT

Historical Figures

```
E  N  I  W  R  A  D  F  T  P  E  P  Y  S  K
H  J  F  N  A  S  N  A  H  U  J  M  E  L  K
M  E  A  O  L  F  H  R  Z  T  R  C  P  E  H
P  N  W  T  E  D  R  A  K  E  I  I  H  L  L
S  N  K  W  I  R  G  D  C  A  I  M  N  M  V
T  E  E  E  G  I  N  A  B  K  N  T  S  G  K
E  R  S  N  H  E  H  Y  E  O  L  N  M  H  C
P  S  M  I  L  F  T  E  P  U  U  E  I  E  K
H  I  T  S  R  U  H  K  N  A  P  D  T  N  B
E  O  O  R  M  V  I  E  A  R  D  S  I  O  G
N  N  G  N  I  M  E  L  F  F  Y  L  E  C  N
S  S  S  H  T  F  F  D  J  B  K  V  A  V  A
O  Z  U  E  C  R  O  F  R  E  B  L  I  W  J
N  B  O  L  E  Y  N  A  I  R  O  T  C  I  V
T  Z  Y  D  C  R  O  M  W  E  L  L  P  G  I
```

ALFRED the Great	Guy *FAWKES*	Samuel *PEPYS*
Mary *ANNING*	Alexander *FLEMING*	Walter *RALEIGH*
Anne *BOLEYN*	*HENRY VIII*	Ernest *SHACKLETON*
BOUDICA	Edward *JENNER*	Adam *SMITH*
Oliver *CROMWELL*	Horatio *NELSON*	George *STEPHENSON*
Charles *DARWIN*	Isaac *NEWTON*	Alan *TURING*
Francis *DRAKE*	Emmeline *PANKHURST*	Queen *VICTORIA*
Michael *FARADAY*	Robert *PEEL*	William *WILBERFORCE*

Meat and Fish

```
P T V M E A T F C F R M Z O A
N W U T C J T G M P U U P W B
M D R O Y O J J R S S P O R K
S Z H F R E D T S A Y N N V U
P I C C K T K E Y L B I N E C
Y E K R U T L Y C M V B E H L
L G P A D S C A Y O S E I S U
O A T B A K J O M N Y C J T B
B S S E A B A S S B K N M E H
S U C J W R J S I E O K E A E
T A A S A R D I N E S S M K S
E S L F J G G Y H D T U D G O
R Z L U W F I S H U O D A U O
E G O T E L L I F C F E E B G
N N P Y T U N A J K G Y Z T T
```

BEEF	HAM	SARDINES
CHICKEN	LAMB	SAUSAGE
COD	LOBSTER	SCALLOP
CRAB	MEAT	SEA BASS
DUCK	MUSSELS	STEAK
FILLET	PORK	TROUT
FISH	RABBIT	TUNA
GOOSE	SALMON	TURKEY

Fruits and Vegetables

```
D T G E E L J L K M K U B C A
B O T A M O T L E E V R P S D
A L N W D S T F U T O V O D S
N G O I N A Y O N C T J U M T
A A L J O G R J C C N U O A R
N R R J E N E O P I O O C N A
A L E M O N L H E F R P S E W
S I L C P I E Y A H O P C M B
P C P U K C C T S T F A A H E
I S P C D H V U A O R M I O R
N E A U G E M T R R E N U S R
A P S M H R O S O A L T U L Y
C A C B A R W T E N E I M Y P
H R G E T Y H B U G B V M P R
M G P R M N C S A E H C A E P
```

APPLE	*GARLIC*	*PEACH*
APRICOT	*GRAPES*	*PEAR*
BANANA	*LEMON*	*PEAS*
BROCCOLI	*LETTUCE*	*PLUM*
CARROT	*LIME*	*POTATO*
CELERY	*MUSHROOMS*	*SPINACH*
CHERRY	*ONION*	*STRAWBERRY*
CUCUMBER	*ORANGE*	*TOMATO*

Kitchen and Tableware

```
K I S F N R E L E E P F I R O
C V A L V K W S G D T U G F E
C Z U W K M E S E S T A O J O
O N C O N K R A V F G A L S P
L E E B J U C L G E I O B P E
A L P S O J S G J H K N T L N
N O A P U A K S C C W S K N E
D R N O M U R G N I K A B I R
E E Y O J W O D N E P R C K B
R S F N Z F C R E I D N L P L
K S A L I K E O P L X O S A E
R A S P A T U L A D T I O N N
O C F H A J K A S W L T M W D
F N S R T E O G D C A V O C E
N F G I V D A O C R I C U B R
```

Cutting *BOARD*	*WOODEN* spoon	*FORK*
BAKING sheet	*SPATULA*	*KNIFE*
CHEF'S knife	*COLANDER*	*SPOON*
PEELER	*SAUCEPAN*	*PLATE*
Can *OPENER*	*CASSEROLE* dish	*BOWL*
BOTTLE opener	*MIXING* bowl	*TABLE*
CORKSCREW	*BLENDER*	*GLASS*
GRATER	*SOUP* spoon	*NAPKIN*

Novels

```
T D T I B B O H T G R E A T D
S C K J R E E M N R S A H F A
F L O W A N E O F E A E N H V
Z M W P V A R A S D R V I A I
E H V R E J K A W U P W E L D
N E E T E N I N D O R J V L F
G C L A R I S S A L M C M H S
G R O S R I D D V C P A E H N
F P E I B T V L P A F R N V Y
P R I N C E K L O P N C I T J
A M M E R C S R D S R I V D Z
L R B O I A Z K H T E E T T E
P Z A R I B M R G L A J R Y E
V B B L M T N E M E N O T A A
V Y B K A D G N I R E H T U W
```

ATONEMENT	GREAT Expectations	The Black PRINCE
BRAVE New World	HEART of Darkness	The Good SOLDIER
BRICK Lane	JANE Eyre	The HOBBIT
CLARISSA	Lord of the FLIES	The WOMAN in White
CLOUD Atlas	NINETEEN Eighty-four	VANITY Fair
DAVID Copperfield	PRIDE and Prejudice	White TEETH
EMMA	Robinson CRUSOE	WOLF Hall
Gulliver's TRAVELS	Silas MARNER	WUTHERING Heights

Herbs and Spices

```
G M O M A D R A C T F O H M T
H J A L L I N A V U S N C M A
P G B C I N N A M O N A N S R
A P A Y L O G L Z Y P G E G R
P R Y R C O E N Z I R E A D A
R B L A N N V T C O D R L R G
I O E M N T Y E U S L O L A O
K C A E H H L N S I Y H Z T N
A U F S Y Y D Y C D E V I S G
H M K O N M I D B P Y L W U M
O I A R M E W Z F A N G O M M
N N U T M E G E K P S E N H D
C F Z J Y R E G N I G I Y I W
T N I M N O R F F A S W L K W
W M S E V I H C S P A L Z U B
```

BASIL	FENNEL	ROSEMARY
BAY LEAF	GARLIC	SAFFRON
CARDAMOM	GINGER	TARRAGON
CHIVES	MINT	THYME
CINNAMON	MUSTARD	VANILLA
CLOVES	NUTMEG	GROUND
CUMIN	OREGANO	WHOLE
DILL	PAPRIKA	SEEDS

Screen Stars

```
W N J O S L M N C N Y J B K B
I Z S Y F M I A E Z M Z B B A
N G I R D L T E H H C N E D A
S I H R P R H I M T P Z L F O
L A C A A S P C Y N A W A H D
E R H W M N G W L D H T B G W
T C E J O R Z O P R R E S A B
Y T D S E Z C E H S L A W N G
S N T G G N G C H T E P H A U
I A O N I G F T E E R L T R I
W R O L I V I E R A C I B B N
W G W P D M N N Y L F P F A N
W Z Y B S M C K E L L E N L E
J A K N I G H T L E Y I W O S
G W Z G K N A M L O C R H Z S
```

Christian *BALE*	Errol *FLYNN*	Laurence *OLIVIER*
Kenneth *BRANAGH*	Hugh *GRANT*	Simon *PEGG*
Charlie *CHAPLIN*	Alec *GUINNESS*	Michael *SHEEN*
Olivia *COLMAN*	Tom *HARDY*	Maggie *SMITH*
Daniel *CRAIG*	Keira *KNIGHTLEY*	Jason *STATHAM*
Judi *DENCH*	Andrew *LINCOLN*	Patrick *STEWART*
Idris *ELBA*	Ewan *MCGREGOR*	Emma *WATSON*
Colin *FIRTH*	Ian *MCKELLEN*	Kate *WINSLET*

People

```
E V I T A L E R Y B Z U C G F
H S N D D Z D S O B B Z U M T
Y H U S B A N D S G A O P R O
A L R O R E P T G M N B Y T D
T U A E P E T U Y I N I F E D
T G F J G S H A S W R W K E L
P S S C U N I T M Y I L M N E
K H N S V N A T O M Z F P A R
F R I E N D E R N R O J E G N
R E T I R E E E T E B O N E G
R K V D A N C T U S R J R R D
E C N A T N I A U Q C A H D L
N U B R V S I S T E R E P P I
J B A G W G N I E B N A M U H
P P C O L L E A G U E C N Z C
```

HUMAN BEING	BABY	FRIEND
HUSBAND	TODDLER	COLLEAGUE
WIFE	PARENT	RELATIVE
PARTNER	CHILD	KING
BOY	ADULT	QUEEN
GIRL	TEENAGER	ROOMMATE
BROTHER	RETIREE	STRANGER
SISTER	ACQUAINTANCE	SPOUSE

Personality Traits

```
E D T R S U O I T A T R I L F
W E L U S U O I T I B M A G O
Y Z A L E D K Y L D N E I R F
H S I F L E S H K E E L M J P
T D D S E E O S B R A V E G G
R E B T R V L P V Y B N S E G
O D A U A F U B O A Y U D N N
W A C B C Y U L A M O D D E D
T E K B U F T J Z I A W O R J
S H T O A S P M T A L I O O C
U G D R E O G U L B H E I U M
R I N N L E A A B L E W R S D
T B O I I C Z V E E D K Y U P
Z H T A L K A T I V E S L I J
O E G C H E E R F U L L D V F
```

AMBITIOUS	FLIRTATIOUS	MOODY
AMIABLE	FRIENDLY	POLITE
BIG-HEADED	GENEROUS	RELIABLE
BRAVE	HONEST	SELFISH
CARELESS	KIND	SHY
CAUTIOUS	LAID-BACK	STUBBORN
CHEERFUL	LAZY	TALKATIVE
DULL	LOYAL	TRUSTWORTHY

Physical Appearance – Face

```
P C A W E T O I E S C J K H B
M S L F Z H F R O W N D A L E
I Z R E U I Y U B L S Z U Z G
F E P B A N S Y S V E E I H I
A P Y S U N H R I L R S D W L
C Z N E D S S N H M I H E E O
E U J H B E H H N K O A H U U
B C V E L R T Y A Z U P C N E
G R L R S Y O N S V S P R E L
J R Z L V O T W I N E Y A B P
H O O K E D N K S O W N R D M
O E I G U Y E S S K P O V K I
V Z Y F G R E E N A U V R B D
A F R E C K L E S N D S I B O
L C R S S I N K D P S G L N O
```

NOSE	FACE	EYEBROWS
BIG	CLEAN-SHAVEN	ARCHED
POINTED	HAPPY	BUSHY
HOOKED	ROUND	EYES
SNUB	SAD	BROWN
DIMPLE	SERIOUS	BLUE
FRECKLES	OVAL	HAZEL
FROWN	THIN	GREEN

Physical Appearance – Body

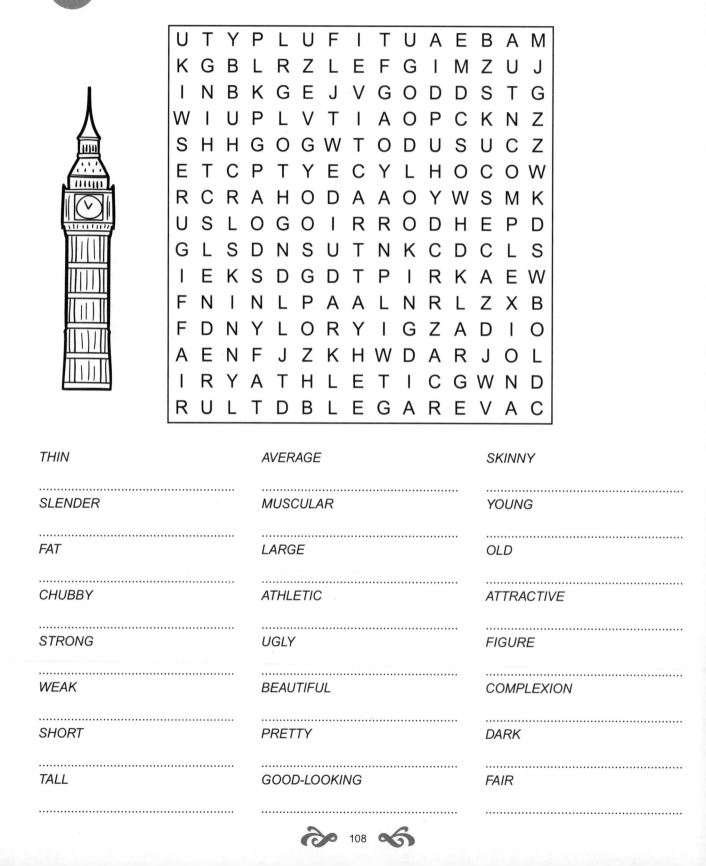

U	T	Y	P	L	U	F	I	T	U	A	E	B	A	M
K	G	B	L	R	Z	L	E	F	G	I	M	Z	U	J
I	N	B	K	G	E	J	V	G	O	D	D	S	T	G
W	I	U	P	L	V	T	I	A	O	P	C	K	N	Z
S	H	H	G	O	G	W	T	O	D	U	S	U	C	Z
E	T	C	P	T	Y	E	C	Y	L	H	O	C	O	W
R	C	R	A	H	O	D	A	A	O	Y	W	S	M	K
U	S	L	O	G	O	I	R	R	O	D	H	E	P	D
G	L	S	D	N	S	U	T	N	K	C	D	C	L	S
I	E	K	S	D	G	D	T	P	I	R	K	A	E	W
F	N	I	N	L	P	A	A	L	N	R	L	Z	X	B
F	D	N	Y	L	O	R	Y	I	G	Z	A	D	I	O
A	E	N	F	J	Z	K	H	W	D	A	R	J	O	L
I	R	Y	A	T	H	L	E	T	I	C	G	W	N	D
R	U	L	T	D	B	L	E	G	A	R	E	V	A	C

THIN	AVERAGE	SKINNY
SLENDER	MUSCULAR	YOUNG
FAT	LARGE	OLD
CHUBBY	ATHLETIC	ATTRACTIVE
STRONG	UGLY	FIGURE
WEAK	BEAUTIFUL	COMPLEXION
SHORT	PRETTY	DARK
TALL	GOOD-LOOKING	FAIR

Physical Appearance – Hair

```
D H Z F B W A B T M A T H U O
L F E T Y E N I F T L Z T B H
A F R Z F Y D M D Y C Z G J I
B J F I D P U C A U L O N G G
I B H U Z Y L C R Z N D E R H
W L T C R Z L L K G I W L E L
S H T B R D Y I M E Z G R A I
B P I H F E N U A E K A E S G
R Y L T G P W A F T L R D Y H
U D B I E I Y C D C Y F L J T
N E L O T B A N U H Y N U R S
E Y O Y Z E B R I T R R O T V
T D N N S Y N O T H D H H P M
T I D S E V C D M S S D S M A
E Z U P J Y N W S S V C J P C
```

CREW CUT	DYED	BRUNETTE
PONYTAIL	FINE	RED
WIG	FRIZZY	WHITE
BALD	GREASY	SHINY
CURLY	HIGHLIGHTS	SHORT
DANDRUFF	LONG	SHOULDER LENGTH
DRY	BLOND	SPLIT ENDS
DULL	DARK	STRAIGHT

English Football Clubs

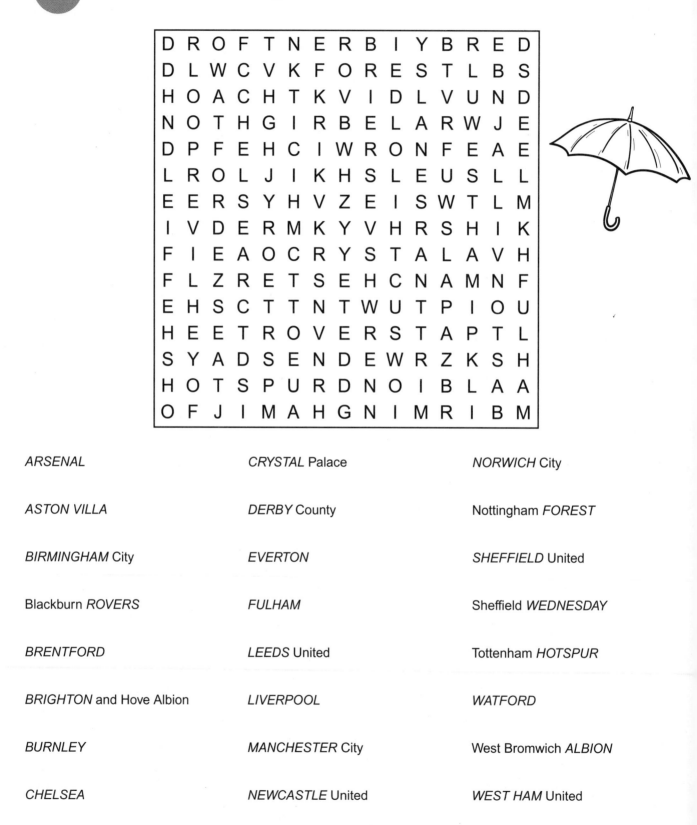

```
D R O F T N E R B I Y B R E D
D L W C V K F O R E S T L B S
H O A C H T K V I D L V U N D
N O T H G I R B E L A R W J E
D P F E H C I W R O N F E A E
L R O L J I K H S L E U S L L
E E R S Y H V Z E I S W T L M
I V D E R M K Y V H R S H I K
F I E A O C R Y S T A L A V H
F L Z R E T S E H C N A M N F
E H S C T T N T W U T P I O U
H E E T R O V E R S T A P T L
S Y A D S E N D E W R Z K S H
H O T S P U R D N O I B L A A
O F J I M A H G N I M R I B M
```

ARSENAL	*CRYSTAL* Palace	*NORWICH* City
ASTON VILLA	*DERBY* County	Nottingham *FOREST*
BIRMINGHAM City	*EVERTON*	*SHEFFIELD* United
Blackburn *ROVERS*	*FULHAM*	Sheffield *WEDNESDAY*
BRENTFORD	*LEEDS* United	Tottenham *HOTSPUR*
BRIGHTON and Hove Albion	*LIVERPOOL*	*WATFORD*
BURNLEY	*MANCHESTER* City	West Bromwich *ALBION*
CHELSEA	*NEWCASTLE* United	*WEST HAM* United

SOLUTIONS

1

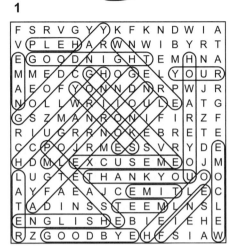

2

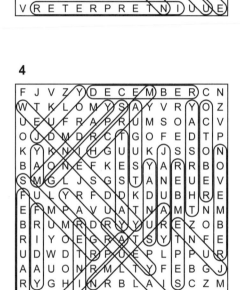

3

4

5

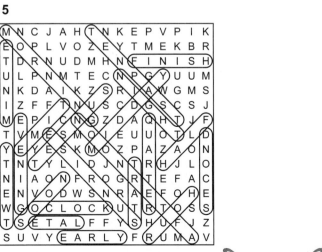

6

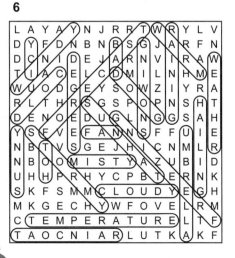

SOLUTIONS

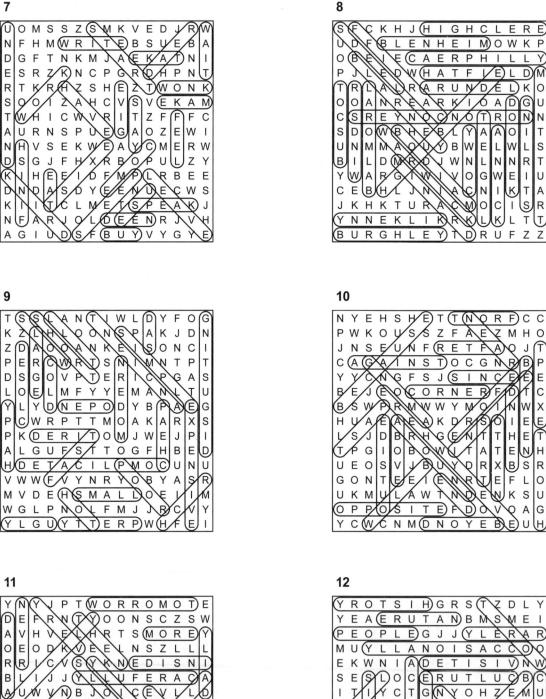

7

8

9

10

11

12

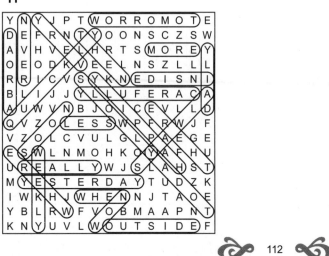

SOLUTIONS

13

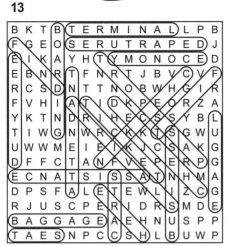

14

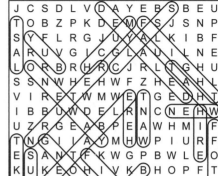

15

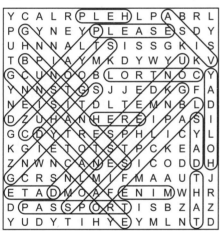

16

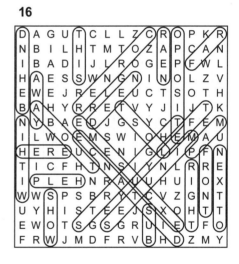

17

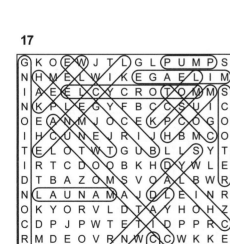

18

SOLUTIONS

19

```
H T V T N E D I C C A H R R V
R R N U C L A E S Z A E Z Y O
K O W N R E G A R A G F V A T
V R O O U J Y W I N M Z K W D
F M D E O P A H A E D W P E Y
J D N N T T Y D C R U Y Z N K
L S E T E K N H N E Y S T O P
Y L K R D C A N O H K Y I Y D
A O O Y V N N P S T C M L F
W W R T I W A A A V P E A R
E D B C S O I L R C T E X H A
V O E T W D A C K T B A E E C
I W E S C A S L I A N O N D J
G N B C J O D H N T A E Y E R
S C I T U R M P G T D A E J J
```

20

```
B K Z S I N G L E L B T B O B
G E B L R L J Y L I M A F N R
Z E R S L E G B I K A F E W E
D W D L G U S R K U B A J E C
A U T B J G F E Q V R N C L O
C F U O E U A R B J I A B M M
C J O S R E L K Y V L G M U M
E O K O M S H F N P A H P O N
S D C R O T R A J E B T S D N
S B E R I H W S F I A S I E D
I N H Y P O U T F J C T O U
B A C O H U T C R R F L E F N
L J U V T S Y B R P I O A B H
E Y M U L E T S O H H T U O Y
G W Y U E S L F O A E P C M D
```

21

```
R A N I T V Y Z T E A V J A D
E F G R E S T A U R A N T O M
T U S W I N F M O C E R U R Z
A U K O A H D L K I F B I B H
E F N F K B E L C Y L I M A F
H H K J T W P A E E E O B U L
B C B B E O L M H P C P R J N
M E K K L D S C P L A E U L
K R D F E N C R E U M M Y N U
K P C D V I H O O L Y Z R V K
E I B E I W L S L W G T D F S
Y L I G S N E N D D S N R G S
T L L M I F G L U Y R S I I W
R O L B O F A I D D V L A S D
Z W H Z N D L K F P S T H P E
```

22

```
Y S M B L K P T L A U N D R Y
A H O W E R E G E S S Y A D E
T O H E I C A T K N T M S O L
S W W C P R G R L I T M M N O
H E E T B G A N C L S A O E P
T R D A P P G I S R V D O A P
B S G B H I R E E A H E R E N
W E J F F T C C K Z O T E N I
H A L U C H Y A P M E A S S I
E K O E G C N W E Z V S E T M
R C L I L C H E O R S T R W M
E E N I I A L A G R O G A V I
C I N E O M C U R I T A A W
W G S J C M R L R R G E O S B S
G D P E Y D L N F R E F B A H
```

23

```
O Y I G Y R G R C A S H H F J
I F A U L T Y V F H J D T W G
L B J C M D Z D F S S H E A R
K R B A R E C E I P T I S E N
I U J S U E E J Z L Z F G Y N
D V V R R D M E Y H N I U N
S N T V E W K I B B A R S G T
F I W H M F N S T H R U T W G
A H W G P G W I C C I T S B G
Y T K T D C F X I W A E W I N
O O C Y P C E J N W Y R R J I
H L B A E F W R A P P E D B K
O C Y N O N F Z H G E E H S O
N B U O B T O P U G B D N J O
O R D M K V U M T E L B F P L
```

24

```
K G A E R U T I N R U F V M H
W K T O B A C C O N I S T O R
Y T T K O M H L L Y W O T P E
R L L G N M I T O Y S H O P L
D E L I C A T E S S E N K G L
N D H P T R B O O K S T O R E
U S G O C K Z F R B B M P O S
A M Y H L E J R B R L H O C H
L C Y S O T A T F A A T A E S
W E A T B R N R R O D E R I
V S V F H E M E M U Z Z T Y F
R H A I E U N A R B A K E R Y
S O L G S E C I F F O T S O P
W E N I G Y S B O U T I Q U E
C U C P E T S H O P B U T T Y
```

SOLUTIONS

25

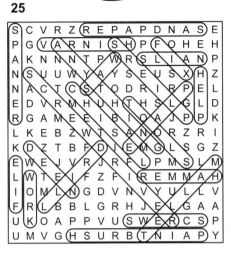

26

27

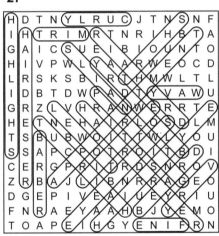

28

29

30

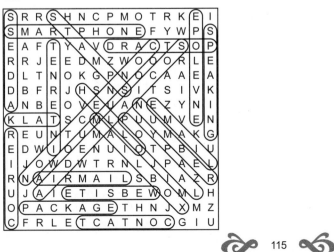

SOLUTIONS

31

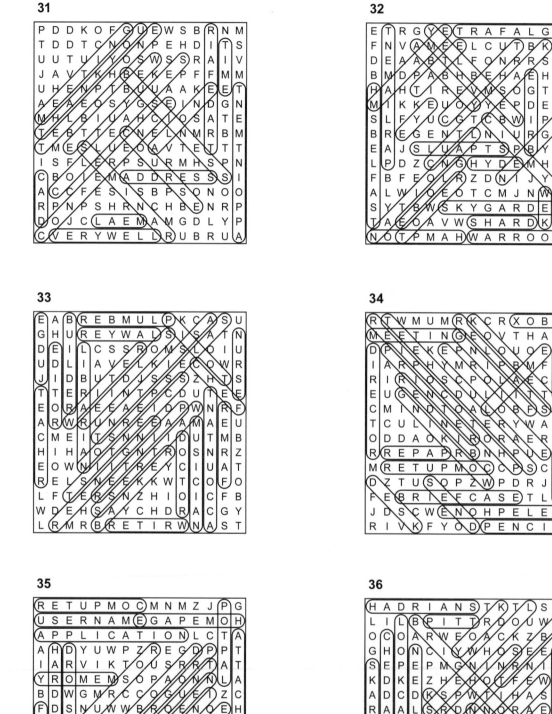

32

33

34

35

36

SOLUTIONS

37

38

39

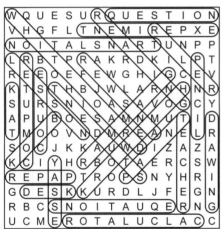

40

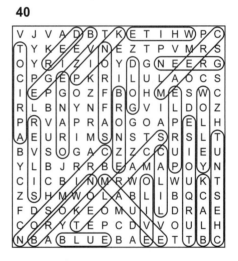

41

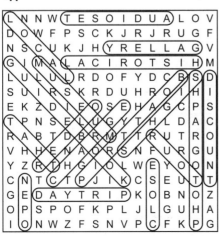

42

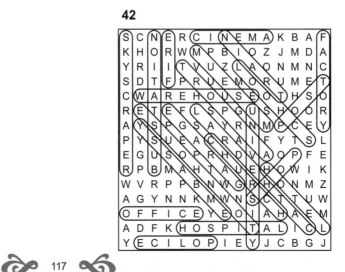

SOLUTIONS

43

```
A L A C I R O T S I H W M M M
B O L R S C A S I N O K L J U
J R L S E T N E M E S U M A S
B P A E P P A R H E W V O R E
R B F A A F O D E C P A K Z U
I G R A Y Z D M I V R K E N M
D K E R P I V D D U U Z Q E Q
G S T T N E M U N O M R H U G
E N A G G E F I L D L I W C A
L I W A K L O O I D Y S H I L
P U B L M T M T R E C N O C L
M R E L R S Z J D B R F V C I
E R A E E A U O T S A O C F V
T J C R A C F T O W N H A L L
C I H Y N I G H T C L U B Y A
```

44

```
V S S A T R A C A N G A M N E
H A S T I N G S Z O T D E T L
W C N A V M R P H L O Y X D I
O I O E D H Z I Z M C C H L Z
C D I R A S W P E A N S I R A
Y U N G P I E S M I W R B O B
T O U F N N D E N A S M I W E
A B R P G A R V L O A S T V T
E L L Y P E N G S I T I O N H
R O I A U S R M E T C I O N A
T S Y S C O A S I O R T A M N
H F E A C K O L Z R V A N J A
I I I V D R A W D E C N F C J
D V U O G E N A M O R I F N R
L O N D O N V Z C G O C A A F
```

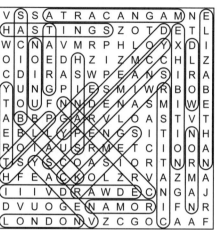

45

```
C S I Y G N O I S S I M D A K
E C N A S S I A N E R U R O I
W K N I E C I H P A R G S M B
G U O E J E V I S S E R P M I
L N I O A U D I O N E R D P S
A R T I B A J C U A E A M H D
U W I N M E Z W L S D E L V T
S V B A R B D L S D E L V T I
U P I F H U V I E A B A D O M
N I H T C O U U J O M I G E R
U F X L S N I T F G O A Z R A
P D E U I E H D S P N A R B
O F W S Z F T W E N G B E P T
H G M P U S H R N H L B P H H
V P Z L A G N V A S W V O S P
```

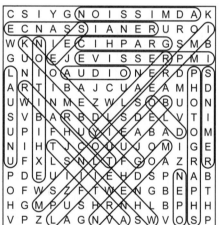

46

```
B T S E B I I E H W B E F N U
C H A I R R R D T S I S D S W
H U Y S G E G B P N K E Y I E
J O A C H V W T E D I N O N T
S F T W C N R A P U N U O B S
E T J Y N R R E M J U S E U I
S C R A A E T B M E W I Z A C
S L O O S Z R I T I F C Z J T
A A O F T N E M E M E C O B H
L L L L G S M G D K P T B J T
G E J L B T I U T O W E L A N
N D A G N N A J P A Z Y H L T
U F E Z G R H O O H W N O L U
S O M C D U L U V I U Z R C B
H P C S K G S U N S C R E E N
```

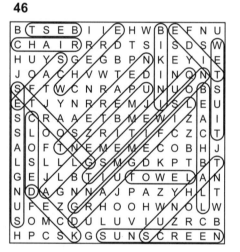

47

```
P F U B R B B S U H B P C W M
D C O D O B I R M D W H H I U
K O U R A E R M E B I I H P E
R R O B M B C G L D H F E G G
Z A Y F U W H D N L J C S G
S B R H K K L V F E M O T E D
B D E W O L L A U P P D R A I
H D E E F T S A E R B O A T H
V T T H A V M O P I Z P T D S
M E N U M M W F R U Z K B T O
E G F G I H I G H C H A I R Y
L Y Y I L C E W G D H U U D L
I L G K Y E L B A T I U S K I
V Y E A R O L D R E J U N T S
D O K S I E N A Z F Y P V V D
```

48

```
L A K L E Y I I V U H M F S F
K E D S M N G K C I T S E S P
Y C L P I C T V H M T N G P Z
D T U B M E W R O F O R U I A
Z D I G I A N O A T M L I D P
D N I L B S R Z S N I A D E R
P L E H I H S E N A C D E A I
V S E U T B L E R F A E D S A
S M T A J B A D L B C A E H C
F E B A B E N S C Z E G H L E
R F F O I A D J I J A R U C L
A Z C Z H R B A G D E A I T E
M I I N K B S Y B S J R C U R H
E C N A T S I S S A T R W C H
Z D E L B A S I D V P J O C W
```

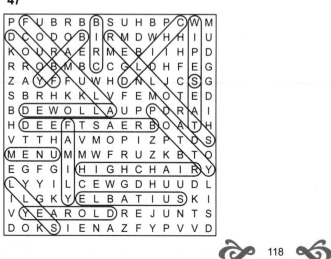

118

SOLUTIONS

49

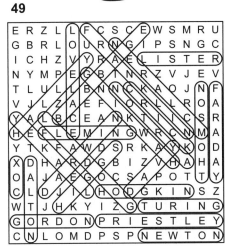

50

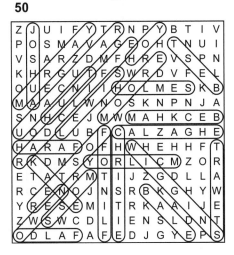

51

52

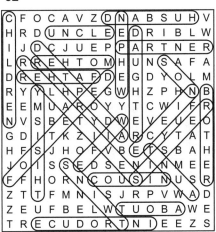

53

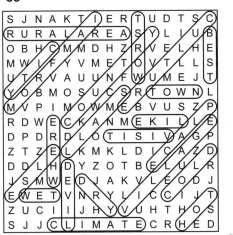

54

SOLUTIONS

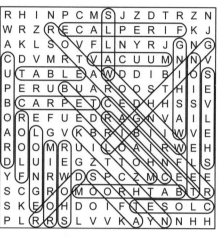

55

```
E G A T T O C E E T V U Z T A
S K Y A Z Y N S N G C O R K D
W V L F G E Z T O G G A D J R
R D I E D B C Y L F D S L O D
V T M R R N G L A I T R O Y W
L L A M S B E E T E E M O H B
O G F W M B R I P D M E J B T
F U A F Y P O Y E A V S C G N
W T T R J N I V T G N U T A E
T J Z S A J I E N Y E O M R M
S O P L I L S L V O W H O A T
A B O U T D D T A I G T D R A
Y Y R M S D E C O R A T E E P
E F J P P S K A H J G L R W P
A B R S M O O R D E B E N K A
```

56

```
R H I N P C M S J Z D T R Z N
W R Z R E C A L P E R I F K J
A K L S O V F L N Y R J N G G
C D V M R T V A C U U M N N V
U T A B L E A W D D I B I O S
P E R U B U A R O O S T H I E
B C A R P E T C E D H H S S V
O R E F U E D R A G N V A I L
A O L G V K B R I B I W V E H
R O O M R U I L O A I R W E H
D L U I E G Z T T O H N F L S
Y F N R W D S P C Z M C E E E
S C G R O M O O R H T A B T R
S K E O H D O I F T E S O L C
P L R R S L V V K A Y N N H H
```

57

```
W M C E G K S D K Z N E H Z P
T A I M A W L D G Y K U A Z C
O O H S A T E W P C K S I J O
O F A S G Z W S O T C S R A N
T B I D E T O T S H O I B T D
H S R H L I T R H Y M T R O I
B C D W S O R S O B B A U O T
R R R E N A P T W R Z D S T I
U U Y A O O W V E O R K H O O
S B E H N D Y H R L L I P N N
H F R G Z R O U T M I H H M E
A W E R E L B R G U T O P E R
C O O P M A H S A A O A T T O
E L I F L I A N B N O M M E B
S C I S S O R S P S T K U C J
```

58

```
S U G U I V H S S T G Z R D Z
E D C D K C B H S S V E S R I
S R V M N W O A U S N G S C B
N E M U N W F V W N T S T E P
E S L Z E K R E I H O N C H H
L T E O E M T V A F G M F E L
C D R H G T K H E B P E A M P
A B D R E E S A R E T L A Z C
T G F P U A P U E K A W L T S
N O D P O R M L N K B Y V R K
O G B O F P S F R N A R T A C
C U I M G A N O C Z A I F I O
S C H O O L W R E I P A I N L
I J Y W S H S A W Y W H O M E
```

59

```
Y Y U R P R G Z L N E G H N T
A H C L Z M W M R I E O I I Y
S W R O N G E Y I H R M O R E
Y P A G Y T Z S Z I G E C T P
L D G A W A J S R E A K V B O
E F H J H H H B S U E I Z U S
T D O P J W H T H E O A E O S
U P O I N T E U R T L C I D I
L E Z D N D Y V H E H Z F K B
O G A W E L O G P W Y G N O L
S E V B T Z T N J A R I R X L
B U Y C D U Z I O T H S O R E
A A A A H H A O A T U N J D V
M X B T D S B G R R E S A C V
E N J V S O S S E U G C O R A
```

60

```
E L E C T I O N U I V G C K R
R E T S I N I M E M I R P G O
Y F M A U V P N O I G I L E R
R R G P T F I N P E A C E N G
Y E T F R C T L E Y K F U D K
R A P S L I B U S Z G K M E C
M U J A U R S B N E I R P R R
E M S U P D E O O L R T E J I
D I L B P F W T X T I A C N M
I C S C I E N C E A N W L C S
C I F Y E N O M T N S U A A O T
N L E T H N I C I T Y L R E S
E E M P L O Y M E N T L O C H
T N E M N R E V O G P T J V P
```

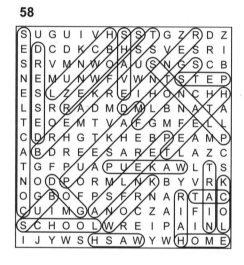

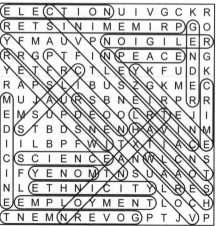

SOLUTIONS

61

62

63

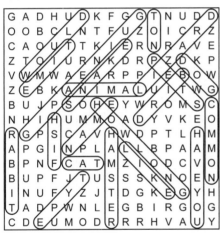

64

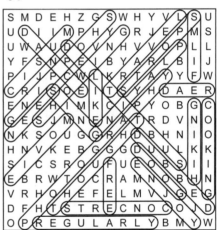

65

66

SOLUTIONS

67

68

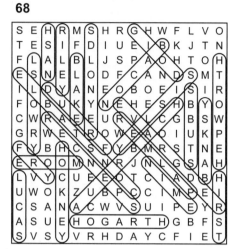

69

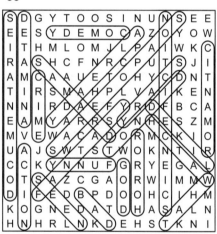

70

71

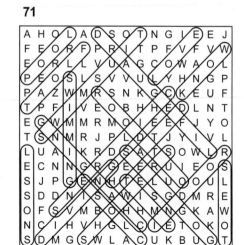

72

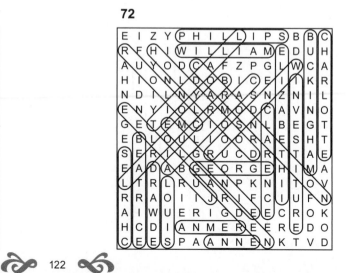

SOLUTIONS

73

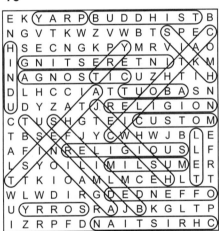

74

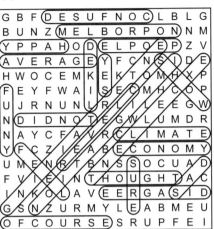

75

76

77

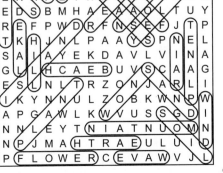

78

SOLUTIONS

79

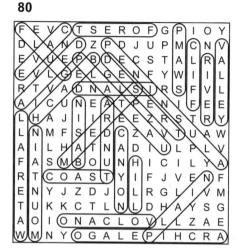

80

81

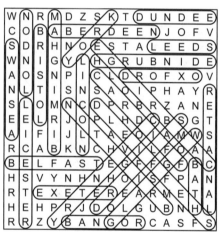

82

83

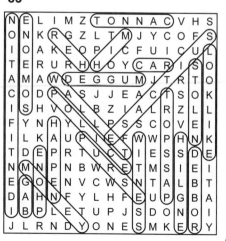

84

SOLUTIONS

85

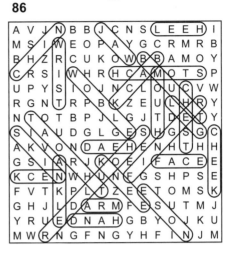

86

87

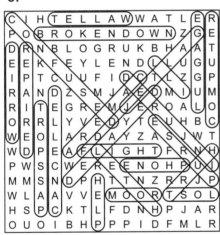

88

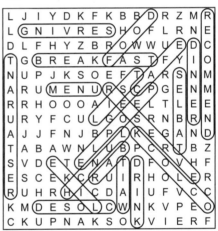

89

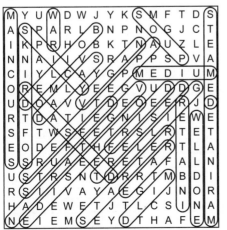

90

SOLUTIONS

91

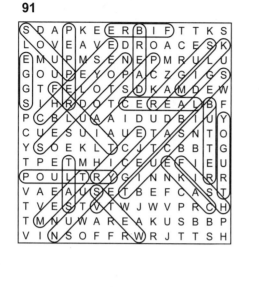

92

93

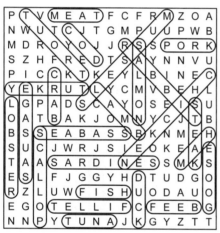

94

95

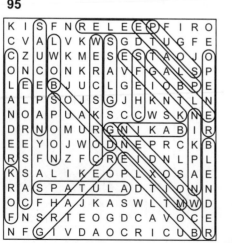

96

SOLUTIONS

97

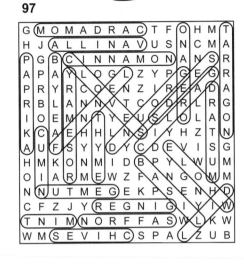

98

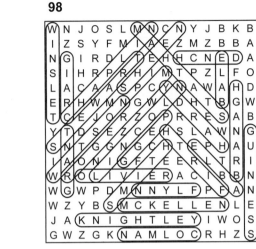

99

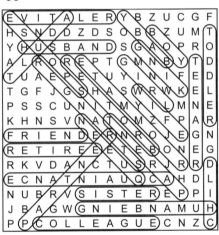

100

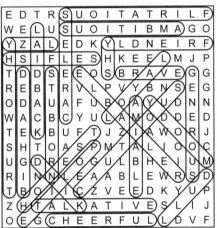

101

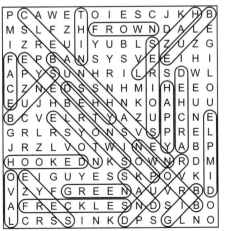

102

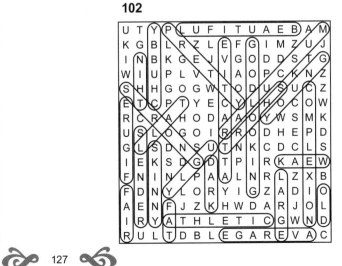

SOLUTIONS

103

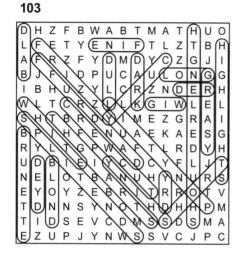

104

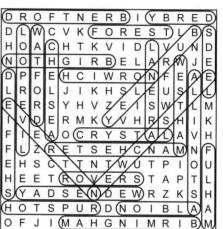